P9-CFW-193

TEST WORDS YOU SHOULD KNOW

1,000 Essential Words for the New SAT and Other Standardized Tests

P.T. Shank

Adams Media

Avon, Massachusetts

Copyright ©2006, F+W Publications, Inc.
All rights reserved. This book, or parts thereof, may not be reproduced
in any form without permission from the publisher; exceptions are
made for brief excerpts used in published reviews.

Published by
Adams Media, an F+W Publications Company
57 Littlefield Street, Avon, MA 02322. U.S.A.
www.adamsmedia.com

ISBN 10: 1-59337-521-2
ISBN 13: 978-1-59337-521-8
Printed in The United States of America.

J I H G F E D C

Library of Congress Cataloging-in-Publication Data
Shank, P. T.
Test words you should know / P.T. Shank.
p.   cm.
ISBN 1-59337-521-2
1. Vocabulary tests--Study guides. 2. SAT (Educational test)--Study guides. I. Title.

PE1449.S457 2006
428.1--dc22
2006014704

This publication is designed to provide accurate and authoritative information with
regard to the subject matter covered. It is sold with the understanding that the publisher is not engaged in rendering legal, accounting, or other professional advice. If
legal advice or other expert assistance is required, the services of a competent professional person should be sought.
—From a *Declaration of Principles* jointly adopted by a Committee of the American
Bar Association and a Committee of Publishers and Associations

Many of the designations used by manufacturers and sellers to distinguish their
product are claimed as trademarks. Where those designations appear in this book
and Adams Media was aware of a trademark claim, the designations have been
printed with initial capital letters.

This book is available at quantity discounts for bulk purchases.
For information, please call 1-800-289-0963.

Contents

Dedication

To Christine Marie Merkel Nessel.
Because really, to whom else would I dedicate my first book?

Acknowledgments

Even I cannot find the words to truly thank the people who made this book happen. Shanna, the greatest editor ever; Don, without whom this book simply would not have been written; Mitchell and Ed for the use of their basement; Miss Phyl for keeping me fed and answering the phone; everyone who came up with a sentence or asked "What does that mean?" when a definition still wasn't clear enough; and finally C. Rex Mix and Betty Witt for instilling in me the love of words I carry with me to this day—I thank you.

Introduction

In this day and age, words are perhaps more important than ever before. We are no longer just communicating with our neighbors, friends, and coworkers. Today, with Internet, e-mail, and even global businesses, we are communicating with people from all over the country, all over the world. One thing hasn't changed, however. The words we choose to express ourselves continue to be the strongest representation of who we are as individuals. Being able to express ourselves articulately continues to be one of the best ways we can present ourselves as intelligent, well-educated people.

Okay. Great. But how will this book help you? If you are studying for the SAT or the GRE standardized tests, the answer is relatively obvious. Every word in this book has been identified as one that you might encounter in the verbal sections of one, if not both, of those tests. Even if you are not studying for a standardized test, these words will increase your vocabulary and assist you in presenting yourself well.

This is the fourth book in the excellent Words You Should Know series by Adams Media. It follows a similar pattern as its predecessors. There are five parts to this book. The body of the text includes over 1,000 words that have a strong possibility of appearing on a standardized test. These words are defined in easy-to-understand language that won't leave you more confused than when you started. A pronunciation guide that actually makes sense and a sentence using the word correctly accompanies each entry. Along with the words, within the main body of the text, you will find helpful hints about word usage, definitions, and common mistakes. At the end, we have also provided a list of the words themselves as an easy reference.

The second part of the book is an exercise section. Following the exercises is an appendix on word roots. These are helpful if you should run across a word on the test or in other reading that you don't know. Often, understanding its root and being able to break down the word is enough to allow you to understand the new word within the context of the sentence. After the roots, you will find three more appendices that offer more information not only on many of the 1,000 words in the book, but other words as well. Words that mean something other than what you expected. Words that are commonly misused. Even some words that are not actually words at all, in spite of their regular use in everyday conversations. This section offers some helpful hints to help you prepare for the SAT and GRE. Wondering what you'll do if you just don't know a word? Concerned about improving sentences or dealing with antonyms? Intimidated by the thought of a timed essay? Be sure to keep reading after the book is "done." These are appendices you really don't want to skip or ignore.

So what makes this book different from the other Words You Should Know books? The words in this book range from those that are probably refreshers for high school students to words that a professional who's been out of school for over a decade might never have run across. Also, we have made a concerted effort to ensure there is very little overlap among the words in *Test Words You Should Know* and the three previous books in the series. Most of the words in this book you will not find in the other three, which makes it both a great standalone guide and a perfect companion piece if you already have one or more of the others. If you are in high school and want to increase your SAT scores or if you have been out of high school longer than you want to admit and simply want to learn a new word or two, I believe you will find words that challenge you and, hopefully, enjoy this book.

Yes, I said enjoy this book. Because words should be and can be fun. That's one of the hardest concepts for some people to grasp, and yet it is true. The more fun you can have with words, the easier it becomes to remember them and use them correctly. The goal of this book, as with its predecessors, is to help make words—even words for a standardized test—fun and easy to use. So, whether you are studying for a test or for yourself, may you come to enjoy the book and the words.

abbreviate (a-BREE-vee-ate), verb
To shorten or condense by omitting letters or words
These days, not many people realize R.S.V.P. was originally used to abbreviate the French phrase "répondez s'il vous plait," meaning "please reply."

aberrant (aa-BER-ant), adjective
Unusual from accepted or expected norms; unexpected in light of past behaviors
The girl knew her brother wanted something because of his aberrant friendly behavior.

abet (AH-bet), verb
To assist or urge another person, usually to do something illegal; to help commit a crime
She was shocked to learn that by simply driving him to the airport, she had abetted in the commission of a crime.

What I Meant to Say Was . . .

Often, words look and/or sound almost identical, especially if you are unfamiliar with them. Abet (AH-bet) and abut (uh-BUT) can easily be confused, especially when you are reading quickly. Abet means to aid someone in a criminal act, and abut means to border or be on the edge. Remember to read carefully to catch words like these!

---

abeyance (uh-BAY-ens), noun
A temporary halt to an activity; a short suspension
The presentation was in abeyance until the technical problems could be resolved.

abjure (ab-JOOR), verb
To recant, take back, or publicly give up previously held thoughts, opinions, or beliefs
Thomas More's refusal to abjure his Catholic beliefs eventually cost him his life.

A

ablution (ab-LOO-shun), noun
The act of washing oneself usually for a ritual or as part of a religious rite
The surgeon considered scrubbing up not only hygienic but an act of ablution that helped prepare her mentally for her work.

abridge (uh-BRIJ), verb
To shorten a text without changing the meaning of the document
Over the years, many students have appreciated others' ability to abridge some of the longer literary works required in English classes.

abrogate (AB-ruh-gayt), verb
To cancel or remove by a person of authority
So many officers had abused the power of the position, it was finally abrogated and the authority for decisions split up among several different departments.

abscond (ab-SKOND), verb
To run away; to leave in a hurry and in secret to avoid detection or arrest
The plan was to abscond with the money and retire drinking margaritas on the beach.

abstemious (ab-STEE-mee-us), adjective
To actively avoid being self-indulgent, especially when eating or drinking
After a particularly wild night, he decided to be more abstemious in the future when it came to alcohol.

abstinence (AB-sti-nans), noun
The practice of avoiding certain specific behaviors
Some health professionals believe that encouraging abstinence while teaching about condoms is a legitimate and effective way to reduce the spread of STDs.

abstract (AB-strakt), adjective
Not based in fact or absolute existence; based in thought, idea, or theory
He prided himself on the fact that his students not only learned names and dates but could also grasp more abstract concepts by the end of the term.

abstruse (ab-TROOS), adjective

Confusing; not easy to understand; muddled and unclear

The dean thought the professor's teaching style was intentionally and unnecessarily abstruse.

abut (uh-BUT), verb

To be next to; to share a border; to come to the edge of something else

They were pleased their new property would abut a national park, so no one could build too close to them.

accede (ak-SEED), verb

To take or rise to office or position of authority; or to agree to a demand

Gerald Ford never dreamed that he would accede to the office of President of the United States.

The police recommended the family accede to the ransom demands.

accessible (ak-SESS-uh-bul), adjective

Easily approached, reached, or entered

The developers knew the plaza had to be interesting, fun, and accessible for the project to succeed.

Similar but Not the Same

Many words are virtually synonymous—their definitions seem identical. However, they cannot always be used in exactly the same way. Just because they are similar doesn't mean they are interchangeable. Acclaim (uh-KLAYM) and accolade (AA-koh-layd) are two of these words. Use the word acclaim when you are referring to words of praise. An accolade, on the other hand, may be words of praise or something more tangible, such as a prize or an award. Be aware of the subtle differences between words that seem the same and you'll be sure to choose the right one.

---

acclaim (uh-KLAYM), verb or noun

To praise loudly (verb) or loud and public praise (noun)

The critical acclaim for her work made her hopeful for an award nomination.

Even other scientists acclaimed his work as the breakthrough that would change the way doctors treated illnesses.

A

accolade (AA-koh-layd), noun
Any word, token, or prize given in appreciation, usually formal
As nice as the official accolade from the school was, his father's look of pride meant more.

acerbic (AA-ser-bik), adjective
Blunt, bitter, and sarcastic, usually regarding a personal attitude or way of speaking
She knew underneath her grandfather's acerbic persona beat the heart of a teddy bear.

acquiesce (ak-wee-ESS), verb
To accept reluctantly but without complaint; to give in
He decided to acquiesce to his girlfriend's request that he wear a suit rather than face her hurt silence.

acrid (AK-rid), adjective
Sharp, bitter, unpleasant; generally describing a taste or smell
The acrid smell throughout the science wing was a telltale sign something had burned in the lab.

acrimony (AK-rhi-mo-nee), noun
Bitterness, anger, bad feelings, usually mutually held
The bride's parents agreed to set aside their feelings of acrimony in order to keep the wedding day peaceful.

acumen (AA-kyoo-men), noun
The ability to make wise decisions in a particular area or profession
He was well-respected, even early in his career, for his obvious business acumen.

adage (AD-ij), noun
A short saying or old phrase that states an accepted truth
Many adages currently in use were originally penned by Benjamin Franklin.

adamant (AD-uh-ment), adjective
Insistent; refusing to change one's mind; determined
Even though the actress was sick, she was adamant about going on with the performance.

admonition (ad-MON-ish-shun), noun

An official warning; a scolding, usually followed by the threat of greater punishment for another offense

The vice principal let the vandal go with detention and an admonition not to do it again or she would be expelled.

adulation (ad-dyoo-LAY-shun), noun

Excessive flattery; deep love and affection

Some public figures become so accustomed to the adulation of their fans that retirement is difficult.

adulterate (uh-DUL-ter-ayt), verb

To lower the quality of something by adding another substance

Her father could never understand why she chose to adulterate her coffee by adding cream and sugar.

adumbrate (AAD-um-brayt), verb

To explain very briefly; to outline the high points

The outline was supposed to adumbrate the research paper.

What I Meant to Say Was . . .

It's a common mistake to mean one word but write or read a completely different one, even if their meanings are not similar. Adversary (AAD-ver-sayr-ree) and adversity (AAD-vers-ih-tee) can easily trip you up. Adversary is someone working against you, and adversity is hardship.

---

adversary (AAD-ver-sayr-ree), noun

Opponent; someone on the other side of an argument or competition

History teaches us that even adversaries can come to respect one another's skills on the battlefield.

adversity (AAD-vers-ih-tee), noun

Trouble; misfortune; difficulty; a time of personal trials and challenges

She considered herself lucky to have had a relatively easy childhood instead of one filled with adversity and hardship.

A

advocate (AAD-vuh-kut), noun or (AAD-voh-kayt), verb

A person who publicly speaks for or on behalf of another (noun) or to speak for or on behalf of another; to argue or speak in favor of something (verb)

As a mother, she knew she must act as an advocate for all children, not just her own.

The panel was moved listening to the doctor advocate for patients' rights.

Which Word?

Many words can be used as either a noun or a verb. Advocate is one of them. The verb to advocate is pronounced (AAD-voh-kayt) and means to speak for and help another person. The noun advocate is pronounced (AAD-vuh-kut) and is the person doing the speaking for and helping of another person. Therefore, an advocate's job is to advocate for his clients. Be sure to pay attention to the context of the word so you don't get the verb confused with the noun!

aesthetic (ahs-THEH-tik), adjective

Regarding beauty and/or enjoyable appearance; pleasing to the senses

For aesthetic reasons, the girls enjoyed having the football team warm up outside their dorm.

affable (AAF-uh-bul), adjective

Friendly; likeable; easy to get along with

His affable nature meant he made friends all over campus even though he was only a freshman.

affirmation (AA-fur-may-shun), noun

A statement or declaration of support or acceptance; a statement of agreement

The student body president's affirmation of the school's new homework policy was necessary for it to pass through the student government.

aggravate (AAG-gruh-vayt), verb

To make something worse; to exacerbate a situation; to annoy or frustrate

Picking at a scab will only aggravate it, not make it heal faster.

aggregate (AAG-gruh-gut), noun
A whole or total, usually made up of unexpected or disparate parts
Individually, the team members were a motley crew of different personalities and temperaments, but taken in aggregate, they were talented and effective.

agile (AA-jyl), adjective
Being able to move quickly and easily; light on one's feet; having quick reflexes
She learned quickly that being agile was her most important asset when babysitting the rambunctious child.

agog (AH-gog), adjective
Eager, excited, in anticipation of
The young woman was agog at the thought of seeing New York City for the first time.

alchemy (AL-khem-ee), noun
The ancient, scientific study of trying to turn one substance into another, specifically metal into gold
The practice of alchemy seems foolish today but it was once considered a legitimate science.

alcove (AL-kohv), noun
A small cut-out or deeper area, usually in a room
The small studio seemed larger than it was due to the alcove for the bed and the large windows that let in light.

alleviate (uh-LEE-vee-ayt), verb
To reduce, lessen, or make less severe
He took yoga classes in order to alleviate stress and improve his overall physical as well as mental health.

aloof (uh-LOOF), adjective
Emotionally cold, distant, or withdrawn
Most people thought he was stuck-up and aloof when really he was just very shy.

altruistic (al-TROO-is-tik), adjective
Selfless; concerned for the greater good
>*The family refused to take their altruistic donations off their taxes because they felt it would demean the gift.*

ambidextrous (am-BEE-deks-truss), adjective
Able to use either the right or the left hand equally well
>*Although I can write my name with my left hand, I am in no way ambidextrous.*

ambiguous (am-BIG-yoo-us), adjective
Having more than one possible meaning or interpretation; unclear and undecided
>*The rules on how to handle an abusive client were ambiguous so the staff members often had to use their own judgment and hope for the best.*

ambivalence (am-BIV-uh-lenss), noun
The state of having strong yet conflicting feelings about the same situation or person
>*Breaking up with him should have been easy but she couldn't get past her own ambivalence about doing so.*

amenable (uh-MEEN-ah-bul), adjective
Responsive to suggestion; able to be swayed to do something
>*The class hoped the teacher would be amenable to giving them another day to work on their research papers.*

amicable (AM-ik-ah-bul), adjective
Friendly, nice; without serious disagreement
>*The landlord hoped to fill the apartments with people who were amicable, relatively quiet, and tidy.*

amorphous (UH-mor-fus), adjective
Without clear shape or form; undefined
>*Everyone involved was thrilled to see a thriving business grow from what started as an amorphous idea.*

A

anachronistic (uh-NAK-kron-is-tik), adjective
Based on another, earlier period in history; out of place in the present time
The idea of being a gentleman may seem anachronistic but many women still appreciate the effort.

analogous (uh-NAL-uh-gus), adjective
Similar to; easily comparable; alike in core ways
Although their backgrounds were analogous, they discovered they didn't agree on many issues.

anarchist (AN-ar-kist), noun
One who believes in, wants, and may work toward a society without government where the individuals are free from societal laws
Many teens consider themselves anarchists but it is usually because they don't understand the ramifications of a lawless society.

anecdote (AN-ek-doht), noun
A short, sometimes amusing retelling of an event
Some of my favorite memories involve sitting listening to my grandfather tell anecdotes about my father's childhood.

What I Meant to Say Was . . .
Words that look or sound almost identical can cause confusion, especially if they are unfamiliar. Anecdote (AN-ek-doht) and antidote (AN-tee-doht) are two commonly confused words. An anecdote is a humorous story, and an antidote is a medicinal cure. Just remember to read carefully!

anomaly (ah-NOM-ah-lee), noun
Something unusual or out of the norm; unexpected based on previous actions or occurrences
Her poor grade on the test was an anomaly considering she was usually the professor's best student.

A

anonymous (uh-NON-uh-mus), adjective
Unnamed; by an unknown person
> *Many authors use pseudonyms because they want to remain anonymous.*

antagonist (an-TAG-ohn-ist), noun
One who is openly adversarial or hostile; an enemy
> *The substitute teacher was easily able to identify both the antagonists and the studious kids in the class.*

antediluvian (an-tee-deh-LOO-vee-ahn), adjective
Old-fashioned to the point of being humorous; traditionally, during the time before the biblical flood
> *The senior partner decided it was time to retire when he realized the younger partners considered his ideas antediluvian.*

antidote (AN-tee-doht), noun
Cure for poison; anything that makes a person feel better
> *Her friends took her out dancing in the hopes a night out would be an antidote for the funk she had been in all month.*

antiquated (AN-tee-kway-ted), adjective
Old-fashioned, often to the point of being obsolete
> *The plumbing in the old building was antiquated and needed to be replaced before the couple could move in.*

antithesis (an-TIH-theh-sus), noun
Something that is in direct opposition to something else
> *The run-down motel was the antithesis of the luxury hotel they had hoped for on their honeymoon.*

apathy (AA-puth-ee), noun
A notable lack of interest, emotional connection, or passion; indifference
> *Many people believe it is voter apathy that causes election turnout to be so low.*

aplomb (uh-PLUM), noun
Self-assurance and grace, especially when under pressure; the ability to handle oneself well in stressful situations

Her friends were impressed with her aplomb when her ex-boyfriend brought a new girl to the party.

apogee (AA-poh-gee), noun
The point in the moon's or a satellite's orbit at which it is furthest from the earth; the climax or culmination of a project or event

He knew presenting his dissertation would be the apogee in his quest to receive a Ph.D.

apostate (ah-PAH-stayt), noun
A person who rejects a religious or political belief

In countries without religious freedom, apostates are usually outcasts.

apotheosis (uh-PAH-thee-oh-sis), noun
The raising of someone to divine status

Even many non-Catholics believe that the apotheosis of Mother Teresa from nun to saint is appropriate.

apparition (aa-puh-RIH-shun), noun
A phantom or ghostlike image

The girls thought they were being visited by an apparition but it was just their brother making shadows on the wall.

appease (uh-PEEZ), verb
To placate, calm, or satisfy a person by meeting his or her demands

He always wore his seatbelt when driving in order to appease his mother.

apposite (AA-puh-zit), adjective
Appropriate for the situation; completely suitable

The woman was relieved she had worn a dress instead of pants as it was apposite for the garden lunch she decided to attend.

A

apprehension (app-ree-HEN-shun), noun
Fear, concern, or anxiety that something bad will occur; nerves or jitters
   New mothers often have a difficult time letting go of their apprehension over having a new baby.

apprise (uh-PRYZ), verb
To inform, tell, or fill in; to bring up to date
   When his parents got to the hospital, they could not find a doctor who could apprise them of their son's situation.

approbation (aa-pro-BAY-shun), noun
Great praise; rave reviews; high compliments and honors, generally formal or public
   Everyone expected great things from the young writer after she had received such approbation for her first book.

arable (AYR-uh-bul), adjective
Suitable or ready for planning and growing plants or crops
   As a city girl, she had no idea if the farmland was arable or not.

arbitrary (AHR-buh-trayr-ree), adjective
Left to personal interpretation; vague and undefined; without strict guidelines
   Due to the arbitrary nature of the coach's instructions, none of the players understood what was expected of them.

arboreal (uh-BOR-ee-uhl), adjective
Living in trees; describing animals living in trees; regarding or having to do with trees
   The rainforest is a good place to see gibbons, sloths, and other arboreal creatures.

archaic (ar-KAY-ik), adjective
Very old-fashioned; from an earlier point in history and no longer in use
   Before judging the past, we must remember that in 1,000 years what we now consider normal will be considered archaic and out of date.

ardor (AR-dor), noun
Emotional heat or passion; passionate, often overwhelming love
I admit I was amazed by the ardor in my grandfather's old letters to my grandmother.

argot (AR-go), noun
The language or slang used by a specific group
Her most difficult adjustment in college was no longer using the argot of the streets where she had grown up.

arid (AYR-id), adjective
Very dry; desert-like, often used to describe climate
It is important to stay hydrated when visiting arid climates, or you risk a number of unpleasant physical problems.

arrant (AYR-unt), adjective
Complete and total; unarguable; plainly obvious
She couldn't understand why her son missed the arrant logic in finishing his report early instead of putting it off until the last minute.

arrogance (AYR-uh-ganz), noun
A sense of being better than others; exaggerated pride
Underdogs are often inspired to play better by the arrogance of higher ranked teams.

articulate (ar-TIH-kyu-lut), adjective
Able to speak clearly and express one's thoughts well; well spoken
He resented people's surprise that he was articulate when they learned he had grown up in the inner city.

artifact (AR-tih-fakt), noun
Something made by humans that has historical or archeological importance
The museum hosted a display of priceless artifacts from the early third century.

artisan (AR-tih-zen), noun
Someone skilled in making crafts by hand
Although I had heard his mother was talented, I didn't realize she was such an artisan until I saw her woven baskets.

ascendancy (AH-sen-den-see), noun
Position of power; superiority, or dominance
Many sociologists believe Japan's ascendancy in the global arena is inevitable.

ascetic (EH-set-tik), noun or adjective
A person who rejects nearly all physical comforts and lives a bare, Spartan life, usually for spiritual development or devotion (noun) or living a life of self-denial, usually for spiritual development or devotion (adjective)
Not many people can handle the sacrifices required to become an ascetic.
The monks' lives were ascetic but happy.

asperity (ah-SPEHR-i-tee), noun
Harshness, roughness, or nastiness of manner; irritability
No one was shocked by the asperity in her voice when she talked about the teacher who had given her a failing grade.

aspire (ah-SPYR), verb
To dream; to hope to achieve; to set as a goal
He aspired to be a great hockey player from the first day he put on skates as a five-year-old boy.

assiduous (ah-SIH-joo-us), adjective
Having great attention to detail; consistent and diligent; overly aware of details
A research assistant must be assiduous in weeding out fact from fiction, finding missing details, and meeting all deadlines.

assuage (ah-SWAYJ), verb
To ease; to make something less painful or severe; to relieve a desperate need or desire
Even apologizing was not enough to assuage her guilt over making such a stupid, insensitive comment to her friend.

astringent (uh-STRIN-jent), noun
A solution that causes skin or other tissue to tighten or contract
A good astringent may help clean pores and keep skin healthy.

astute (uh-STOOT), adjective
Being able to read a situation and figure it out accurately; being able to read between the lines
An astute therapist will read a client's body language and not just listen to what is said.

asylum (ah-SIY-lem), noun
Protection and safety offered by a government, church, or other ruling body
Many refugees from war-torn countries seek asylum in the United States.

atonement (uh-TOHN-ment), noun
Payment, through action, for an injury or harming another; an action that repays a debt
The principal required the students who spit on the floor to stay late and scrub the floors for both punishment and atonement.

atrophy (AA-tro-fee), noun
To weaken and deteriorate though lack of use
The new mother was afraid her intellect would atrophy after spending the first year at home with her children.

attribute (uh-TRI-byoot), verb or (AA-tri-byoot), noun
To credit a particular source or cause; to cite the source (verb) or a specific characteristic or trait (noun)
The young man preferred to take credit himself rather than correctly attribute his jokes to his grandfather.
A sense of humor is the best attribute one can have in a stressful situation.

audacious (aw-DAY-shus), adjective
Bold and adventurous, sometimes recklessly so; without concern for the normal or expected
The comedian's audacious jokes shocked people as often as they made people laugh.

A

augury (AW-gur-ree), noun
An omen or sign of things to come; a foretelling of future events
In the theater, a bad final rehearsal is seen as an augury for a good opening night.

austere (aw-STEER), adjective
Severe and strict; without any frivolous additions; intentionally plain and without character
Her austere style kept her from being effective in such a relaxed group.

authoritarian (uh-THAW-rih-tayr-ree-uhn), adjective
In favor of complete obedience; demanding of obedience to the exclusion of individuality
The greatest threat to an authoritarian government is an independent, thinking populace.

autocrat (AW-tuh-krat), noun
A leader with complete and unlimited power
Throughout history, every autocrat has eventually become power-hungry and corrupt.

autonomous (aw-TAWN-uh-mus), adjective
Having the ability to work and exist independently
He quickly discovered his assistant was not autonomous but instead needed daily direction.

auxiliary (awg-ZIL-ah-ree), adjective
Helpful, giving assistance; held in reserve in case extra assistance is required
The auxiliary troops stationed in Germany hoped they would not be needed in the war.

aver (uh-VER), verb
To declare as fact; to swear as true
Witnesses are asked to aver that they will tell the truth in court or face charges of perjury.

aversion (uh-VER-shun), noun
A strong dislike or feeling of disgust; repulsion
While she was no longer afraid of spiders, she still had an aversion to them and knew she always would.

A

Watch Out!

The parts of speech can be changed for many words by simply adding a different suffix. It seems obvious that kind and kindness are related words. Unfortunately, it is not always that simple. Be aware that although aver and aversion appear to be different forms of the same word, they really are not. To aver (uh-VER) means to swear something is true. Aversion (uh-VER-shun) means a strong dislike. Be careful not to get the two confused.

avert (ah-VERT), verb
To change or prevent; to turn away
The young woman used the scary part of the movie as an excuse to avert her eyes and cling to her date.

aviary (AY-vee-ayr-ree), noun
A large structure for housing birds
The zoo aviary was closed for repairs after the storm ripped through the netting.

avow (ah-VOW), verb
To state openly and without shame
He was brave enough to avow he was Republican in a city where most people were Democrats.

axiom (AHK-see-um), noun
A statement that is considered to be true or a given without needing further proof
It is an axiom that people want jobs that pay well and make them happy.

baleful (BAYL-ful), adjective
Threatening; intending to intimidate or cause harm
The baleful look she gave her little brother only confirmed for her parents that he was telling the truth about her sneaking in after curfew.

balm (BAHLM), noun
An ointment used for soothing or healing; anything that causes a pain or hurt to be eased; something that gives comfort
After the breakup, listening to classical music was a balm for his broken heart.

banal (BAY-nul), adjective
Ordinary to the point of boring; dull and uninteresting
Although parents still hire them, most children find clowns banal and childish.

bask (BAASK), verb
To relax and enjoy warmth, either literally or figuratively
After the long, cold winter, all they wanted to do was bask in the Caribbean sun.

beatify (BE-ah-taf-fy), verb
To idolize above all; to make someone blissfully happy
Her friends wouldn't let her beatify her ex but kept reminding her how annoying he could be.

bedaub (beh-DAHB), verb
To smear, usually with something sticky
The groom's attendants decided to bedaub the steering wheel of the getaway car with honey as part of the joke.

beguile (bee-GYL), verb
To charm, often by being deceptive
The young woman didn't have to beguile men because she was naturally friendly and outgoing.

belie (bee-LYE), verb
To be false or misrepresent; to be intentionally inaccurate
The condition of the house belied her claim that no one had come over while her parents were out.

benefactor (BEHN-uh-fahk-tor), noun
Someone who gives money to help a person or cause
Without a generous benefactor, the small art gallery would have gone out of business years ago.

benevolent (beh-NEHV-oh-lent), adjective
Concerned with performing good or charitable acts; being kind and helpful
The teen's benevolent acts throughout the year inspired the whole community to help the less fortunate during the holidays.

benign (beh-NIYN), adjective
Harmless; gentle; without cruel intent or ability
The owners assured people the dog's nature was completely benign but it was hard to believe considering how mean it sounded when it barked.

berate (bur-AYT), verb
To scold harshly; to yell, usually implies an extended scolding
His father berated him not just for cheating on his English test but because the young man was smart enough to not need to cheat.

bewilder (bee-WIL-der), verb
To confuse; to puzzle a person
By the end of the drive, the poor directions and the winding roads had bewildered us.

blandishment (BLAN-dish-ment), noun
Gentle flattery used to get someone to behave in a certain way
She knew better than to try blandishment on her father just to get the car keys because he would just laugh and hand her bus fare.

blatant (BLAY-tent), adjective
Open and in-your-face to the point of being offensive
The teacher was shocked by the blatant cheating going on during the test.

bleak (BLEEK), adjective

Cold, miserable, barren; without hope

Unless she started taking her classes seriously and raised her GPA, her outlook for graduating on time was bleak.

blighted (BLY-ted), adjective

Diseased; given over to hopelessness and despair; sickly; run down

For years after the factory closed, the small town looked blighted with the boarded up windows and empty storefronts.

blithe (BLIYTH), adjective

Lightheartedness to the point of indifference or uncaring; happily uncon-cerned and oblivious

There is something uplifting about watching the blithe play of young children.

boisterous (BOY-stuhr-us), adjective

Cheerfully loud and out of control

The party grew boisterous as more people arrived to help celebrate.

bolster (BOL-ster), verb

To shore up ; to build up; to increase support

The candidate needed to bolster his support in the Midwest if he was going to win the election.

braggart (BRAG-ert), noun

One who boasts or brags unnecessarily; one who builds himself up in order to appear impressive

He had a reputation as a braggart, which people found so annoying it kept them from admiring his skills as much.

breach (BREECH), verb

To break through; to violate

Anyone who has seen water breach a levee will never forget the sight of the flooding or the damage it caused.

brevity (BREHV-ih-tee), noun
Shortness and clarity in written or spoken word
She aimed for brevity in her speeches so she wouldn't bore her audience since she herself hated to listen to speakers drone on and on.

brittle (BRIT-tuhl), adjective
Hard but fragile and easily broken or damaged
The older a woman gets, the more brittle her bones will become unless she exercises and gets enough calcium in her diet.

broach (BROHTCH), verb
To bring up, as a suggestion or topic of conversation; to approach a topic
He finally got up his nerve enough to broach the possibility of a date with her while they were instant messaging.

bucolic (BYOO-kawl-ik), adjective
Idealized characteristics of the country and country life; rustic and pastoral
The bucolic paintings of the farm had made her want to move there but the reality made her miss the city.

bumptious (BUMP-shus), adjective
Loud and self-serving to the point of being obnoxious
Instead of charming and witty, the candidate just came off as bumptious whenever he was working without a script.

buoyant (BOY-ant), adjective
Lighthearted and happy; or able to float
Her buoyant personality brought much needed cheer to the residents of the nursing home.
The buoyant rubber duck was enough of a temptation that the child was finally willing to get in the bath in order to "swim with the duckie."

burgeon (BUR-jun), verb
To increase rapidly; to flourish and grow
The artists were surprised at the burgeoning popularity of their cartoon on the Internet.

burnish (BUHR-nish), verb
To make something smooth and shiny by rubbing or polishing it
Every Sunday, her grandmother burnished the silver before setting the table.

buttress (BUH-tress), verb
To support or reinforce a building, thought, idea, or argument
He had plenty of documentation to buttress his claims in the debate but his opponent's style won over more of the audience.

cabal (kuh-BAHL), noun
A secret group of plotters or conspirators
The Founding Fathers were actually just an articulate cabal with good connections.

cacophony (kah-KOFF-ah-nee), noun
A harsh, jarring, disconnected group of sounds; discordant noise
The cacophony of the horns and sirens during rush hour traffic is enough to give anyone a headache.

cajole (kah-JOL), verb
To persuade someone to do something through persistent flattery, teasing, and/or repeated requests
She hoped to cajole her parents into letting her go to the party after the game, even though it was past her normal curfew.

calculated (KAL-kyoo-lay-ted), adjective
Done with a full understanding of the consequences; carefully examined and planned
He took a calculated risk when he mortgaged the house to pay for her education but it paid off when she graduated top of her class.

callow (KAL-oh), adjective
Inexperienced, immature, naïve; emotionally young
Teenagers from small towns tend to be far more callow than teens from inner cities.

calumny (KAL-um-nee), noun
Slander; a false statement made intentionally to damage another's reputation
The calumny and insults spouted during the debate just made both candidates look bad.

camaraderie (kahm-ah-RAH-duh-ree), noun
Friendly, powerful emotional bonding between people; group trust
The camaraderie formed among sorority sisters is more valuable than the status gained by pledging.

candid (KAN-did), adjective
Completely truthful; not posed; with nothing held back
The teacher waited until she knew none of her students could hear her before she gave a candid opinion of her colleague.

candor (KAN-dohr), noun
Sincere and honest expression of thought or opinion
Although some people were put off by her candor, most people appreciated knowing she would be honest with them.

canon (KAN-non), noun
The general principals, standards, or rules by which something is judged
Societal canon requires a certain code of conduct in public, regardless of what is acceptable in private.

capacious (kuh-PAY-shus), adjective
Roomy; spacious; large
Although her capacious purse looked somewhat silly, it could carry everything she needed for the baby and herself.

capitulate (kah-PITCH-yoo-layt), verb
To surrender or give up; to give in
The babysitter found it easier to capitulate to the child's demands than listen to him cry while his parents were out.

C

captious (KAP-shus), adjective
Tending to nitpick or find fault; overly critical of small mistakes
   The students knew their papers had to be perfect because the professor was a captious grader.

cardiologist (kar-dee-AHL-oh-jist), noun
A doctor who specializes in the heart
   After her grandfather's heart attack, she made a point of meeting the cardiologist who would be handling the follow-up.

carping (KAR-ping), verb
Complaining or nagging in a fault-finding way; unfairly and vocally dissatisfied
   Throughout the trip, their teenagers kept carping about how bored they were in spite of their parents' attempts to cater to teenage interests.

castigation (KAS-tih-gay-shun), noun
A harsh scolding or verbal punishment
   She avoided her father because she knew she deserved the castigation she would get for drinking and driving.

catalyst (KAT-ah-list), noun
Something that causes an event or change without participating in the change or changing itself
   A free press has often been the catalyst needed for people to overthrow an ineffectual or dictatorial government.

Don't I Know That Word?

Sometimes you think you know a word and its definition—and you probably do know one of its definitions. Cataract (KAT-uh-ract) is probably one of those words. You may have heard the word cataract used in relation to an eye or vision problem. That is its most common definition. However, if you double-check the listing in the book, you'll discover it is also a raging waterfall.

cataract (KAT-uh-ract), noun
A great, rushing waterfall
   Although it was a beautiful place for a picnic, the roar of the cataract made conversation impossible.

caustic (KAW-stik), adjective
Sarcastically nasty; biting; mean
   The coach was fired in large part because of the caustic comments he made to his team about its abilities.

censorious (SEN-sor-us), adjective
Quick to cast blame; highly critical and judgmental of others
   The girl would have been more popular if she hadn't been so censorious and had accepted others as they were.

Which Word?
Many words can be used as either a noun or a verb. Censure (SEN-shur) is one of them. The verb to censure means to hand down an official reprimand or scolding. The noun censure is the official reprimand or scolding. So, one could say that Congress may censure a representative by issuing a censure. Be careful not to confuse them.

---

censure (SEN-shur), noun or verb
A strong, official reprimand (noun) or to reprimand formally (verb)
   The legislature issued a censure to the senator for lying under oath during the hearings.
   The school censured the speaker because his presentation had been racist.

centurion (SEN-tyur-ee-ahn), noun
An ancient Roman commander, traditionally in charge of 100 troops
   For Halloween, he dressed as a centurion and carried action figures to represent his 100 soldiers.

certitude (SUR-tih-tood), noun

The absolute certainty that something is true; complete confidence in the truth of a matter

The four-year-old knew with certitude that Santa Claus had been on the roof that Christmas Eve.

charlatan (SHAR-luh-tun), noun

A con artist or fraud; someone who claims to have a special skill that he or she does not have

In the old days, charlatans traveled from town to town to find their next victim, but now they just use the Internet.

chary (CHAR-ee), adjective

Wary; cautious; on guard

Since she was chary about walking home by herself after dark, she never took the shortcut through the parking lot.

circuitous (sur-KYOO-uh-tus), adjective

Roundabout or indirect; winding

Although the walk through the park was circuitous, it was prettier than going directly home so the young couple often took the path when they weren't in a hurry.

clairvoyant (klayr-VOY-ant), adjective or noun

Having the ability to see or know something that cannot be seen or known with the five senses (adjective) or a person who claims to have the ability to see or know something that cannot be seen or known with the five senses (noun)

The old woman who claimed to be clairvoyant did seem to know things no one else did.

The clairvoyant was the amusement park's biggest moneymaker after dark.

clarity (KLAYR-rih-tee), noun

Clearness in speech, appearance, or thought

The lecturer explained her ideas with such clarity that the audience was able to understand the very difficult concept.

cliché (KLIH-shay), adjective

Trite, unoriginal, or overused

The movie plot of aliens attacking the earth and humanity fighting them off has become so cliché I'm surprised any studio still makes those films.

coalesce (ko-ah-LESS), verb

To bond or come together; to form a single unit

The coach loved watching a group of kids come together as strangers at training camp and coalesce into a real team by the season opener.

coddle (KAH-dul), verb

To baby, pamper, or indulge; to treat more gently than necessary

Much to his annoyance, his grandmother still coddled him as if he was a child even though he was a teenager.

coercion (KOH-her-shun), noun

The act of using violence or the threat of violence to bring about desired results

When the businessman couldn't be bought, the mafia tried coercion to get him to sell his property.

coeval (KOH-ee-vahl), adjective

Being of the same time period or era; existing at the same time

It is hard to believe that a man as clean-cut as Elliot Ness was coeval with a man as dangerous as Al Capone.

cogent (KOH-jent), adjective

Clear, concise, and convincing, usually of an argument or point of view; logical and well-presented

Instead of becoming emotional, she presented a cogent argument for getting a new car as a graduation present, and her parents agreed.

cogitate (kah-jih-TAYT), verb

To think over carefully; to ponder and consider; to weigh all aspects of a situation

The state representative had to cogitate on whether he would run for national office because he refused to make a snap decision.

C

cognizant (KAHG-nih-zant), adjective
Aware of; having knowledge about
    Youth today are far more cognizant of the hardship that comes with being an adult than kids of earlier generations.

coherent (KOH-heer-ant), adjective
Able to make sense, be logical; consistently logical
    She chose not to drink often because she stopped being coherent after only one glass of wine.

collaborate (koh-laa-bur-AYT), verb
To work together or jointly, usually to create something
    The writer and the artist decided to collaborate on a children's book.

colloquial (kuh-LO-kwee-uhl), adjective
Used in ordinary speech; informal; may imply regionally used words and phrases
    Many freshmen have a difficult time switching from colloquial language to formal writing in their college research papers.

What I Meant to Say Was . . .

Look out for words that look or sound similar but have very different meanings. Combustible (khum-BUS-tih-bul) and comestible (kuhm-EHS-tih-bul) can easily be confused, especially when you are reading quickly. Combustible means something that can catch fire; comestible means something that can be eaten. Read closely so you don't misread these words.

---

combustible (khum-BUS-tih-bul), adjective
Able to catch fire and/or burn easily
    Smoking while filling a gas tank is not recommended because gasoline is highly combustible.

comestible (kuhm-EHS-tih-bul), noun or adjective

Anything that can be eaten (noun) or edible; fit for human consumption (adjective)

He really didn't impress anyone by referring to the groceries as comestibles.

Travelers to third-world countries need to make sure the food is comestible or it can make them very sick.

commemorate (kuh-MEM-or-rayt), verb

To honor or mark an occasion with a celebration, ritual, or ceremony

The United States commemorates the attacks on the World Trade Center with a moment of silence every September 11.

compassion (kum-PASH-uhn), noun

The awareness of and sympathy for other's sufferings; kindness toward others less fortunate

Even after she became successful, she never forgot the compassion of the people who had supported her during the hard times.

compile (kum-PYL), verb

To gather information from several sources in order to collect in one place

He compiled the names of all the fraternity brothers from the last fifty years in order to invite them to the reunion.

complacency (kum-PLAY-sen-see), noun

The feeling of being so good one doesn't have to try any longer

After acing three tests in a row in the class, a dangerous sense of complacency set in and she stopped studying.

complacent (kum-PLAY-sent), adjective

Smugly content; confident to the point of not caring

Even the best football team will lose a game if the players become complacent.

complaisance (kum-PLAY-sens), noun

A willingness to do what others want; the willingness to go along with the crowd without complaint

Her natural complaisance made her an easy target for manipulation.

C

complement (KOM-pluh-ment), noun
Something used to enhance or perfect another

His dry sense of humor was the perfect complement to her goofy personality.

What I Meant to Say Was . . .

It is easy to confuse words that sound the same, especially when their spellings are also very similar. Complement (KOM-pluh-ment) and compliment (KOM-pluh-ment) are two easily confused words. A complement is something that enhances or improves another, but a compliment is a nice thing to say about someone. Be careful not to mix up these words.

---

compliance (kum-PLIY-uhns), noun
The act of observing and following directions, requests, or advice

The doctor assured her that compliance with the new diet and exercise regime would help her lose weight.

comport (kum-PORT), verb
To behave or conduct oneself in a particular manner; to act in a certain desirable way

She decided to comport herself with absolute dignity in order to counter the rumors she was a party girl.

composure (kum-POH-shur), noun
Being calm and in control of oneself and one's emotions; a calm state of mind

Her ability to maintain her composure during a crisis made her an excellent police officer.

comprehensive (cahm-PREE-hen-siv), adjective
Total; complete; all encompassing; leaving nothing out

After the fire, the insurance company wanted a comprehensive list of belongings that had been destroyed.

compromise (KAHM-pro-miz), noun or verb
A settlement in which the parties all give up some of their demands (noun) or to settle a situation by having all parties give up some of their demands (verb)

The compromise they reached was that she could stay out until one in the morning but she had to call at midnight.

Since she wanted a quiet beach vacation but he wanted nightlife, they decided to compromise and take a cruise.

concede (kuhn-SEED), verb
To reluctantly admit something is true

After seeing the movie, he had to concede that the director could indeed handle a big-budget film.

conceit (con-SEET), noun
Arrogance; an unreasonably high opinion of oneself

His conceit in the interviews was not backed up by his performance once he got the job.

conciliatory (kon-SIL-ah-toree), adjective
Meant to appease someone or make someone feel better

Her conciliatory remarks were not enough to undo the damage caused by the young man's rude behavior.

concise (kun-SIYS), adjective
Expressing a lot of information in a few words

The assignment was to keep the essay to fewer than 200 words so the students could learn to be clear and concise.

concord (KAHN-kord), noun
Agreement and harmony between people or groups

If the original settlers had not learned to live in concord with Native Americans, the settlement would have died out within the first year.

concur (kuhn-KUR), verb
To agree or share an opinion

She hated to concur with her little brother's opinion on anything, but this time he was indeed right about her dress being unflattering.

C

condense (kun-DENS), verb
To make shorter or reduce in volume without losing the meaning of the original subject matter
He had to condense an hour-long presentation to fit the thirty-minute time slot.

condescending (kohn-di-SEN-ding), adjective
Having a superior and patronizing attitude
The seniors regretted being so condescending to the juniors once they were treated the same way by the college students.

conditional (kun-DISH-ahn-ul), adjective
Dependent upon something else; needing other conditions to be met
Her attending the dance was conditional on her finishing her chores and homework on time.

condone (kun-DOHN), verb
To overlook or even support an action without comment or complaint
Many school officials believe if condoms are available in the high schools, the students will believe the adults condone premarital sex.

conflagration (kon-fla-GRAY-shun), noun
A very large, very destructive fire; uncontrollable fire
The paints and chemicals in the garage turned what could have been a small, easily contained fire into a conflagration.

confluence (KAHN-floo-ens), noun
The meeting, joining, or flowing together at one point, originally used in relation to streams
The confluence of John Adams' determination, Benjamin Franklin's vision and Thomas Jefferson's eloquence led to the thirteen original colonies declaring themselves independent of England.

conformist (kun-FORM-ist), noun
A person who behaves only in ways that are socially acceptable and expected
Although he sneered when he called his sister a conformist, he was secretly jealous of her popularity.

confound (kuhn-FOWND), verb
To confuse or puzzle; to mix-up; to be unable to distinguish
No matter how often he drove the route, the directions continued to confound him.

congeal (kun-JEEL), verb
To jell or curdle; to coagulate; to form a loose solid
The dessert was supposed to have congealed around the fruit but it stayed liquid and runny because he used more water than called for in the recipe.

congenital (kun-JEN-ih-tul), adjective
Relating to a condition or characteristic had since birth, usually referring to a disease or deformity
She was still very young when she learned to take care of her congenital diabetes on her own.

congregation (kahn-grih-GAY-shun), noun
A large gathering, often but not always of people for the purpose of worship
The senator's inauguration party brought in the largest congregation of politicians the town had ever seen.
The church's congregation was small but determined to keep the church open in spite of the current financial difficulties.

conjoin (kon-JOYN), verb
Attach, come together, join
The little boy was thrilled when he was able to conjoin two of the puzzle pieces.

connoisseur (kahn-uh-SOOER), noun
A person with great knowledge and training in matters of taste
The butler was, by necessity, a connoisseur of wine and cuisine.

consensus (kun-SENS-us), noun
General agreement; the opinion of the majority of the group
The student government had come to a consensus that they would approach the principal about opening the parking lot to students.

C

console (kun-SOL), verb
To lessen sorrow or grief; to ease emotional pain
   Her friends were unable to console her when she was rejected by her first choice of schools.

conspicuous (kun-SPIK-yoo-us), adjective
Obvious; standing out; unhidden
   He left his report card in a conspicuous place so his mother would find it and see his improved grades.

consternation (KOHN-ster-nay-shun), noun
Extreme dismay or anxiety, usually caused by something unexpected occurring
   The principal's consternation at the break-in was eased somewhat when she learned none of her students had committed the crime.

constraint (kon-STRAYNT), noun
Physical, emotional, or logistical restraint; a binding, literally or figuratively
   A feeling of constraint filled the room as people tried not to react too harshly after the speaker made an inappropriate comment.

constrict (kun-STRIKT), verb
To tighten or make narrower; to close in
   Jitters caused his throat to constrict before every performance but he always relaxed once he started singing.

contemptuous (kun-TEMPT-choo-us), adjective
Showing or having the feeling that someone or something is inferior or worthless
   Although he tried not to be contemptuous of homeless people, he didn't always succeed.

contend (kun-TEND), verb
To claim or assert; to struggle against
   The prosecutor expected the defense to contend the evidence was irrelevant.

C

contentious (kun-TEN-shus), adjective
Argumentative or likely to cause an argument
Her contentious attitude made it more difficult for the group to come to an agreement.

contiguous (kun-TIG-yoo-us), adjective
Touching, connected, or sharing a border; uninterrupted; continuous
Often, stores will ship to the contiguous United States but not Alaska or Hawaii.

contract (kun-TRAKT), verb
To shrink or make smaller
The doctor knew the boy's head wound wasn't too bad when his pupils contracted in the light.

contrite (kohn-TRYT), adjective
Feeling sorry or apologetic
He couldn't stay angry at his sister when she was so contrite for spilling her drink on his homework.

contumacious (kun-tuh-MAY-shus), adjective
Willfully and intentionally rude and disobedient
Although she had been contumacious in front of her friends, she dropped the brave front when she was at the police station by herself.

convention (kun-VEN-shun), noun
Social norms; usual and expected behavior; that which is approved of and accepted by society at large
Female suffragettes defied convention by marching and protesting for the right to vote.

convergence (kun-VER-jens), noun
The act or process of coming together or meeting at one point or place
America's independence from England was largely a result of the convergence of great minds and brave hearts.

C

conviction (kun-VIK-shun), noun
A strong, firmly held belief
    His moral convictions about the importance of all human life caused him to oppose the war.

cordial (KOR-jul), adjective
Warm and friendly; welcoming; nice
    Her mother-in-law was so cordial, the new bride felt comfortable immediately when she arrived at her husband's childhood home.

cornucopia (kor-neh-KOH-pee-yah), noun
A symbol, literally or figuratively, of abundance, wealth, and plenty; when literal, usually in the form of a horn overflowing with fruits and vegetables
    The dean of the law school was a cornucopia of legal information and knowledge.

corporeal (koh-POR-ee-uhl), adjective
Of the body; regarding the body
    A good doctor understands the connection between mental health and corporeal health.

correlate (KOR-uh-layt), verb
To show or prove connection, relationship, or similarity
    Sociologists claim it is easy to correlate high school drop out rates to the rise in crime committed by teenagers.

corrode (kor-ROHD), verb
To rust or be eaten away by chemical reaction; to destroy slowly and systematically
    It was painful for the couple's friends to watch the trust between them corrode as they moved toward divorce.

corrugated (kor-uh-GAY-ted), adjective
Shaped into ridges and grooves
    The boys discovered corrugated steel was good for making the walls of their fort.

counterfeit (KOUN-ter-fit), adjective, noun, or verb
Fake; imitation; made to look like the original (adjective) or a fake; a copy
of something valuable, usually made to defraud or fool (noun) or to make a
copy of something valuable with the intent to defraud (verb)
*She wore counterfeit jewels so people wouldn't know she had been forced to sell
the real ones.*
*Upon closer examination, the Monet painting supposedly discovered in the
family's attic was actually a counterfeit.*
*Printers had become so advanced that it was relatively easy for criminals to
counterfeit money, so the government changed the design on the bills.*

countervail (kown-tehr-VAYL), verb
To offset the effect of something with an equal but opposing force; to counter
*The moral of many stories is that good must countervail evil in order for
humanity to live in peace and harmony.*

covet (KUV-it), verb
To want or desire something that belongs to another person
*The young woman had always coveted her grandmother's pearls so was
delighted to receive them as her birthday present.*

cower (KOW-er), verb
To shrink or cringe in fear
*The puppy cowered away from new people at first but adjusted within a few
weeks.*

crass (KRASS), adjective
Crude and unrefined, usually used to describe a person or attitude
Women found his attitudes about gender roles crass and outdated.

credulity (kreh-DYOO-lih-tee), noun
A tendency to be gullible; ready to believe anything
*The professor's credulity made it wasy for students to get extensions on assign-
ments so long as their excuses weren't too outrageous.*

criterion (kryi-TEER-ee-uhn), noun

A standard or test by which something else is judged or compared

The judges made the criterion for the contest available for all the contestants so everyone would know what was expected.

Goose, Geese, Moose . . . Meese?

Everyone is familiar with adding s or es to the end of a word to make a singular into a plural. However, it's not that easy with some words. Criterion (kryi-TEER-ee-uhn) means one rule or guideline. But when there are two or more rules or guidelines, they are criteria (kryi-TEER-ee-uh). Although many people say "criteria" for both the singular and the plural, it is incorrect to do so. Always read the sentence carefully since "the criterion" and "the criteria" are both correct. The first means there is only one, while the second indicates more than one.

---

cryptic (KRIHP-tihk), adjective

Vague; coded; having a mysterious meaning

Since she didn't know who might hear the message, she made it cryptic enough that only her boyfriend would understand what she meant.

culminate (KUL-min-ayt), verb

To come to the end or completion; to reach the climax of an event or happening

Everyone knew the graduation ceremony would culminate with tears of joy as well as the traditional tossing of the mortar boards.

cursory (KUR-sur-ree), adjective

Brief; without attention to detail; not thorough

In spite of her mother's request, the young woman only gave her room a cursory cleaning before heading out to the mall.

curtail (kur-TAYL), verb

To cut short; to reduce the time or quantity

The concert tour had to be curtailed when the lead singer lost his voice and was given doctor's orders not to sing for six weeks.

D

cynicism (SIN-ih-si-zim), noun
A negative and suspicious attitude; the expectation of the worst
As she got older, it became harder and harder not to let her natural trust of people to turn into cynicism.

cynosure (SIN-uh-shoor), noun
An object or person that has all the attention; the focal point
The new baby was the cynosure of the entire party.

dearth (DERTH), noun
A lack or shortage; not having enough of something
Her sons were pleased that after her trip to the grocery store, there was no longer a dearth of snack food in the house.

debunk (DEE-bunk), verb
To prove false; to disprove exaggerated claims
Medical advances and personal experiences have managed to debunk the earliest claims that cigarette smoking was actually good for you.

decimate (DEHS-ih-mayt), verb
To utterly destroy or ruin; to inflict great damage
The coach taught her team it was better to show good sportsmanship and win with grace rather than try to decimate the other team.

decorum (deh-KOR-um), noun
Appropriate and proper behavior
In spite of his long hair and tattoos, he could act with decorum and dignity when the situation called for it.

defer (DEH-fur), verb
To put off or postpone; to reschedule for a later time
She decided to defer college for a year in order to travel through Europe with her friends.

degradation (deh-grih-DAY-shun), noun
The process of insulting or putting someone down; the state of being put down, insulted, or humiliated
She couldn't bring herself to rush a sorority because she didn't believe in the degradation the pledges went through.

dehydrate (dee-HIY-drayt), verb
To cause something to dry out and lose water
Before hiking or camping, they would dehydrate fruit to carry with them to have as easy snacks.

deign (DAYN), verb
To do something that is believed to be below one's station or dignity
Some of the more stuck-up seniors wouldn't deign to speak to freshmen in spite of being only a few years older.

deleterious (duh-lee-TREE-us), adjective
Harmful or damaging
He studied for every test because he realized that one bad grade would be deleterious to his GPA and lower his chances of getting into an Ivy League college.

deluge (DAY-looj), noun
A great flood or fall of water; anything that overwhelms like a great flood
When the paper leaked that the movie star was in town, the hotel received a deluge of phone calls from people hoping to talk to him.

demagogue (DEHM-ah-gog), noun
A leader who uses the emotions, fears, and prejudices of a populace, rather than logic, intellect, or facts to gain support
Eva Peron, or Evita as she is better known, was one of the most successful demagogues of modern history.

denizen (DEN-ih-zen), noun
A resident or one who is in a particular place often enough to practically be a resident; a native
The denizens of the Bronx have a culture separate from the rest of New York.

dénouement (DAY-noo-mah) or (DAY-nyoo-mah), noun
The final part of a story or movie in which all the loose ends are tied up and all the questions answered
The dénouement of most mysteries occurs when the detective reveals which character is the murderer.

denounce (dee-NOWNS), verb
To declare publicly that something is wrong, evil, or incorrect
After much soul-searching, the senator denounced her own party's stance on immigration.

deplete (deh-PLEET), verb
To use up or greatly diminish in quantity
There is some concern that we will deplete the earth's resources if the population of the planet continues to grow at its current rate.

deplore (dih-PLOHR), verb
To feel strong disapproval; to condemn; to be strongly against
While most people deplore poverty and injustice, few people are willing to sacrifice anything in order to help reduce it in society.

depose (deh-POZ), verb
To remove from office; to remove from power; to dethrone
President George W. Bush sent troops into Iraq to depose the dictator Saddam Hussein.

deposition (dep-uh-ZISH-uhn), noun
A statement or testimony under oath
He didn't have to appear in court because the attorneys were satisfied with his deposition given earlier in the investigation.

deprave (dih-PRAYV), verb
To make wicked; to morally corrupt
She kept a close eye on her teenage son to ensure the influences of growing up in the inner city wouldn't deprave him.

deride (deh-RYID), verb
To ridicule; to speak or treat with contempt; to tease cruelly; to scorn
Under school policy, no student was allowed to deride another for any reason.

derision (duh-RIZSH-un), noun
Mockery, contempt, ridicule
Although many people treated him with derision because of his disability, he had learned to ignore them.

derivative (duh-RHIV-ih-tiv), adjective
Originating from another source; copied or adapted from something else
A paragraph in her essay was so obviously derivative that the teacher feared plagiarism.

descry (duh-SKRY), verb
To finally see; to catch sight of; to figure out through detection
After she turned him down for the third time, he finally was able to descry that she just wasn't interested in a date.

desiccated (DES-ih-kayt-ed), adjective
Dried; dehydrated; having all water removed from
The explorers were not surprised to discover the ancient mummies were desiccated after centuries within the tombs.

desuetude (DEH-sweh-tood), noun
Disuse; inactivity
Rules of etiquette have fallen into desuetude as society has become more relaxed about gender and class roles.

desultory (DES-uhl-tor-ee), adjective
Disconnected; half-hearted; seemingly random
Her presentation was so desultory even her professor realized she hadn't spent enough time preparing it.

detached (dee-TATCHED), adjective
Disconnected either emotionally or physically; separate and apart

Doctors and other health-care professionals need to remain detached from their patients or else they become too emotionally involved.

deterrent (duh-TER-ahnt), noun
Something that discourages or dissuades

For most students, the threat of expulsion is an effective deterrent against cheating on exams.

detrimental (det-treh-MEN-tul), adjective
Harmful; damaging; negative in some way

At this point, everyone knows that smoking is detrimental to a person's health but some people still smoke anyway.

devious (DEE-vee-us), adjective
Sneaky; underhanded

Her little brother could be devious when it came to getting her in trouble and making himself look like an angel.

devise (de-VIYZ), verb
To plan, create, or design, usually referring to the mental process of creation

The city government devised a plan to expand the pedestrian mall in order to bring in more shoppers.

dexterity (dek-STAYR-ih-tee), noun
Skill, ability, or grace, especially physical or mental

Most visitors to the zoo are amazed by the dexterity of the animals in the primate house.

diaphanous (diy-AHF-un-us), adjective
Delicate and filmy to the point of being nearly transparent; gauzy

She had always dreamed her wedding dress would have a cathedral length train and a diaphanous veil.

D

diffuse (dih-FYOOZ), adjective or verb

Spread without specific direction; not concentrated (adjective)

To scatter or spread out; to cause to spread; to thin out (verb)

The diffuse light cast a lovely glow over the evening making the dinner that much more romantic.

The mediator knew he had to diffuse the anger between the couple if he was going to help them come to a mutually satisfying settlement.

digression (di-GRESH-un), noun

A turning away or diversion from the main topic

The students discovered it was easy to distract their teacher with an interesting digression into current events.

dilate (DI-layt), verb

To expand; to make wider or larger

In the dark, our pupils dilate to let in what light is available.

dilatory (DIHL-uh-tor-ee), adjective

Meant to cause delay or postpone; used for the purpose of putting off an event

The young man used a dilatory question to postpone her leaving until he had gained the courage to ask her out.

dilettante (DIL-eh-tahnt), noun

An amateur or uneducated follower of a field of interest, usually the arts; some-one who has an interest in but no real knowledge about a field of interest

His artwork was mediocre at best and would only appeal to the dilettantes at the showing.

diligence (DIL-ih-jens), noun

Persistent and attentive work or effort; determination about one's goals

Her academic diligence paid off when she graduated at the top of her class.

disabuse (dis-uh-BYOOZ), verb

To convince or persuade someone an idea, thought, or belief is false

She hated to disabuse him of his fantasy but she knew his screenplay would never be optioned.

disallow (dis-uh-LOUH), verb

To state something is false; to refute

The police decided to disallow that alcohol had been involved in the accident in order to silence the rumors that the woman had been drinking.

discern (dis-URN), verb

To be able to recognize and understand differences, either visually or mentally

Very young children cannot discern the difference between fact and fiction, so what first appears as lying may actually be the misunderstanding that an event didn't really happen.

disclose (dis-KLOWZ), verb

To share a secret; to make a secret known

It wasn't until the reunion that she was able to disclose she had had a crush on the quarterback when they were in school.

discomfit (dis-KUM-fit), verb

To embarrass or make uncomfortable; to defeat soundly

The couple was so aggressive in their kissing while on the train that many people were discomfited by it.

The football team's goal was to discomfit their last opponent and move onto the state finals.

disconsolate (dis-KON-so-luht), adjective

Deeply sad to the point of being unable to find or accept comfort

She was disconsolate for over a year after her father died.

discordant (dis-KORD-uhnt), adjective

Disagreeing; in conflict; unpleasant or harsh, especially in describing sound

He composed the music to be especially discordant in order to highlight the strife in the scene.

discount (dis-KOUNT), verb

To disregard, see as exaggerated, or dismiss

She was afraid he would discount how important his help had been with her writing the book.

discountenance (dis-KOUN-te-nans), noun
Disapproval

Her expression showed her discountenance even though her words were favorable.

discourse (dis-KORS), noun
A written or spoken communication; a verbal exchange

As the debate team president, he was a master of discourse and could talk rings around most other students and even some professors.

discredit (dis-CRED-it), verb
To damage a reputation; to cause disbelief; to cause another to appear untrustworthy

The candidate hoped to discredit his opponent's positive stance on the environment by proving the other candidate supported deforestation.

discreet (dis-KREET), adjective
Careful; subtle; showing self-restraint

The teachers were discreet about their personal relationship so the students never even knew they were dating.

discrepancy (dis-CREP-uhn-see), noun
A difference between what is stated and what is fact; a difference between facts

The accountant was concerned about the discrepancy between the figures in the books and the amount in the bank account.

discretion (dis-KREH-shun), noun
The ability to act or think responsibly; the ability to act or behave prudently

After his secrets were told all over school, he used greater discretion when deciding who he would confide in.

discriminating (dis-CRIM-uh-nay-ting), adjective
Able to show judgment and distinction; capable of making wise decisions

The socialite was known and respected for her impeccable style and discriminating tastes.

D

disdain (dis-DAYN), noun
Held in contempt; looked down on
The proper, older woman looked with disdain on the fashions of teenagers.

disheveled (dih-SHEHV-uhld), adjective
Messy or untidy, usually used in describing physical appearance
We all knew he had pulled an all-nighter when he showed up to class disheveled and bleary-eyed.

disinclination (dis-in-klih-NAY-shun), noun
Reluctance or unwillingness to do something
Her disinclination to baby-sit on a Friday night was overridden by her need to make some extra money.

disinterested (dis-IN-truh-sted), adjective
Lack of interest or curiosity; being emotionally removed from something
Although he tried to appear enthusiastic, he simply could not hide how disinterested he was in her shopping spree.

dismiss (dis-MISS), verb
To demand or allow someone to leave; or to write off; to consider unimportant or unworthy of attention
The king dismissed the courtiers for the afternoon because he was tired of being surrounded by people.
It is best to simply dismiss e-mail offers as spam rather than be taken in by outrageous claims.

disparate (dis-PAYR-uht), adjective
Essentially different or dissimilar; not easy or even impossible to compare
The two girls' personalities were so disparate, it was hard to believe they were sisters.

disputation (dis-PYOO-tay-shun), noun
Formal debate or argument, often on an academic level
The professor encouraged her students to enter into worthy disputations with her during class but was not interested in wasting time with simple concepts.

D

disquiet (dis-KWIY-eht), noun
A feeling of anxiety, worry, or unrest
   At lights out, a sense of disquiet spread throughout the camp because of the ghost stories that had been told around the campfire.

dissemble (dis-EM-bul), verb
To create or hide behind a fake appearance, attitude, or personality
   It is sad that some young women still feel the need to dissemble instead of being honest about their intelligence and strength.

dissent (dih-SENT), verb
To disagree, usually with a formal or official statement
   It takes courage for a congressman to openly dissent against the party's platform.

dissolution (dis-uh-LOO-shun), noun
The ending of an official organization or body; the breaking up of an established group
   The dissolution of the band was caused by budget cuts in the school's music department.

distend (dis-TEND), verb
To cause swelling or expansion from the inside
   Severe malnutrition causes the stomach to distend in addition to causing other major physical conditions.

distraught (dis-TROHT), adjective
Deeply agitated; emotionally upset
   The girl was distraught until the animal shelter called with the news they had found her lost puppy.

divergent (diy-VER-gent), adjective
Dividing off from a common point; moving in different directions from a single starting point
   Although the brothers had similar interests growing up, they took divergent paths once they graduated.

divest (diy-VEST), verb

To deprive, usually the power or rights of another person

The black majority was divested of their basic human rights in South Africa during apartheid.

divulge (diy-VULJ), verb

To share or make known a secret or something else private

She waited to divulge the fact that she was pregnant until she had told her family first.

doctrine (DOK-trihn), noun

The beliefs or principles held and taught by some governing body, usually political or religious

Most people agree with parts of a political party's doctrine but not necessarily every aspect of it.

document (dok-YOO-ment), verb

To supply written proof; to keep a paper trail

The employees had to document their gas mileage to be reimbursed for it.

dormant (DOR-ment), adjective

Having physical vital signs slowed dramatically; waiting to be roused

Many plants become dormant in winter, blooming again in spring.

dubious (DOO-bee-us), adjective

Uncertain; causing doubt; questionable

Her excuses were always dubious but her teachers never caught her in an outright lie.

dupe (DOOP), verb or noun

To deceive or trick someone (verb) or a person who has been deceived or tricked; someone easily fooled (noun)

The class decided to dupe the substitute teacher by pretending one of the students was deaf.

Her trustworthy nature made her an easy dupe for con artists.

duplicity (doo-PLIS-ih-tee), noun
A state of being two-faced or deliberately deceptive
> *She couldn't stand the duplicity required to juggle more than one boyfriend at a time.*

earthenware (UR-then-wayr), noun
Pottery made from a specific, porous clay
> *The earthenware plates combined with the heavy pewter flatware gave the table a rustic, welcoming look.*

eccentric (ek-SEN-trik), adjective
Following a different, unusual path; straying from the norm or that which is expected
> *The opera singer was as famous for her eccentric style as she was for her singing abilities.*

eclectic (ih-KLEK-tik), adjective
Drawing from or combining elements from many places or situations; multifaceted
> *Many people were surprised at how eclectic his musical tastes were as they encompassed classical and house and everything in between.*

edacious (eh-DAY-shus), adjective
Voracious; greedy for; devouring
> *After months in isolation, the prisoners were edacious for news from the outside world as well as nutritious food.*

edible (EHD-ih-bul), adjective
Able to be eaten; fit for consumption
> *Although the hungry hikers ate it willingly, the rest of us found the burned stew barely edible.*

educe (eh-DOOS), verb
To bring out or draw out; to coax
> *Her goal as a dance instructor was not just to teach ballet but to educe a sense of self-confidence in all her students.*

efface (eh-FAYS), verb
To erase or rub out
The years had not managed to efface the memories of the fabulous summer she had spent in Europe with her friends.

effervesce (ehf-fer-VES), verb
To bubble up; emit small bubbles
The little girl was fascinated by the way the seltzer would effervesce as her grandfather poured it into their glasses.

effete (eh-FEET), adjective
Worn out; out of date; lacking effectiveness; or overly refined, pretentious; characterized by affectation
The teaching style of rote memorization was proven to be effete and so was replaced long ago.
The male actors in the college had a largely undeserved reputation for being shallow and effete.

efficacy (eff-ih-KASEE), noun
Effectiveness; the ability to create the desired effect
The efficacy of the drug was called into question when only half of the test patients responded well to treatment.

effulgence (ef-FOOL-jens), adjective
Bright and radiant; glowing
The effulgence of her personality lit up every room she entered.

egotism (EE-gah-tizm), noun
An inflated sense of self-worth; a tendency to only speak or care about oneself
The artist's egotism eventually gained her a reputation for being difficult to work with and lost her several job opportunities.

egress (EE-gres), noun
The exit; the path out
During the evacuation, all the roads were open for egress so there were no roads leading into the city.

elated (ee-LAY-ted), adjective or verb
Joyous; extremely happy (adjective) or to make joyous or extremely happy (verb)

> *Everyone in the family was elated when she received her acceptance to the college of her choice.*

> *Being nominated for the award elated the scientist because it meant his work was finally being recognized.*

elegy (EL-eh-gee), noun
A poem or song written in honor of someone who has died

> *It was common for bards and poets to compose elegies at the death of a monarch.*

Similar but Not the Same

Many words have definitions that seem identical, but they cannot always be used interchangeably. This is the case for elegy (EL-eh-gee) and eulogy (yoo-LEH-gee). An elegy is a song or poem written in honor of a person who has died. This song may be written by anyone, at any time after the person's death. A eulogy, however, is a statement or speech made about a person who has died. Traditionally, the eulogy is given by someone who knew the deceased at the time of his or her death.

---

elicit (ih-lih-SIHT), verb
To draw out, usually a response from a person

> *The verdict of guilty elicited both cheers and cries of outrage from the large crowd that had gathered outside the courthouse.*

elusive (eh-LOO-siv), adjective
Difficult to find, discover, or capture; just out of reach; unable to be grasped

> *To this day, some people believe the Loch Ness Monster to be a hoax while others believe it to simply be an elusive and crafty being.*

emaciate (ih-MAY-see-ayt), verb
Make abnormally thin, usually due to starvation or illness

> *The need to be accepted and beautiful causes many young women to emaciate themselves in order to look like the models in magazines.*

embellish (em-BEL-ish), verb

To decorate with ornamentation; to add to; to make more colorful or decorative

The urge to embellish a story to make it even more interesting is one every author must fight, especially when speaking with friends.

embezzle (em-BEZ-uhl), verb

To take or steal, usually money, that has been entrusted to one's care

No one knew exactly when the president of the company had decided to embezzle the payroll funds but they quickly realized it had been going on for years.

emblazon (em-BLAY-zen), verb

To display obviously; to put something somewhere it cannot be missed

The student body decided to emblazon the front doors with a welcome sign for the visiting dignitaries.

emend (ih-MEND), verb

To alter or edit with the intent to improve

The teacher asked for rough drafts so she could emend any glaring mistakes that might count against the students' final papers.

emollient (ih-MOL-yent), noun

Any substance that softens or soothes the skin

Lotion with aloe is an excellent emollient, especially during the dry months of winter.

empathy (EM-puth-ee), noun

The ability to identify, understand, and share the feelings of another

A therapist who can balance empathy with objectivity is usually more effective than one who is strictly clinical.

empirical (em-PEER-uh-cul), adjective

Based on verifiable facts rather than theory; fact based

The students had to complete an empirical study on sunscreens with varying levels of protection for an easy summer assignment.

emulate (EM-yoo-layt), verb

To imitate or copy in a flattering way; to strive to be like

Her goal was to emulate Angelina Jolie in fashion, personality, and beauty.

encomium (en-KOH-mee-um), noun

A formal speech or statement in praise of someone

The dean fought back tears while reading the encomium at the professor's retirement celebration.

encumbrance (ehn-KUM-bruhns), noun

A burden; something that makes another thing more difficult

At first she thought watching her little sister three days a week would be an encumbrance but she quickly came to enjoy the time they shared.

endorse (en-DORS), verb

To give or declare public approval; to give backing to; to support

The candidate hoped her stance on fair employment practices would convince the trade unions to endorse her.

engender (ehn-JEN-dehr), verb

To cause, usually a feeling; to bring into existence

Watching his wife and new baby engendered such love in him for his family that it sometimes took his breath away.

engrave (en-GRAYV), verb

To etch or mark permanently; to carve into something hard

The sterling silver award was engraved with his name and the date he won the competition.

enhance (en-HANS), verb

To intensify or increase the value, beauty, or look of something

The sunlight shining on her hair only served to enhance her natural beauty.

enigma (eh-NIG-mah), noun

A puzzle or mystery, usually a person; someone that is difficult to understand

It is a sad fact that women are enigmas to most men and vice versa.

ennui (OHN-wee) or (ohn-WEE), noun
Boredom; lack of interest, usually caused by having nothing to occupy one's time or thoughts
Although the students had looked forward to summer vacation, relaxation quickly turned into ennui as the allure of having nothing to do dwindled.

entangle (en-TANG-gul), verb
To tangle or twist together; to become a tangled mess
She didn't know how she had become entangled in the politics of the sorority but she knew she didn't care for it.

entreat (en-TREET), verb
To ask earnestly; to request wholeheartedly; to plead
The police entreated anyone who had any information about the crime to come forward.

ephemeral (ef-FEM-er-al), adjective
Short-lived or temporary; passing quickly
Although he knew it was ephemeral, he enjoyed the quiet between the time his son left for work and his daughter got home from band rehearsals.

epithet (EP-ih-thet), noun
Phrase used to describe a person, often a nickname picked up by the general population
The late president Ronald Reagan carried the epithet "the Great Communicator" due to his skill at debate and diplomacy.

epitome (ih-PIT-oh-mee), noun
A person or thing that is the ideal all others are compared to
Even so long after his death, many people still consider James Dean the epitome of cool.

equable (EHK-kwah-bul), adjective
Not easily disturbed or agitated; free from extreme emotional highs and lows
His equable nature made him an excellent camp counselor because not even the teenagers could frazzle him.

E

equilibrium (ee-kwi-LIB-bree-um), noun
A state of emotional, mental, or physical balance
The easiest way to keep equilibrium in the house was to ensure the twins received the exact same amount of everything.

equine (EE-kwiyn), adjective
Having to do with horses; relating to horses
His equine laugh was distinctive enough to be identified from anywhere in the room.

equitable (EK-kwit-uh-bul), adjective
Even, equal, or fair
The mediator's job was to ensure the divorce settlement was equitable and both sides came away satisfied.

equivocal (ih-KWIV-ih-cul), adjective
Uncertain; having more than one interpretation, often intentionally in order to mislead
Teenagers will often give equivocal answers when asked about their sex, drinking, and drug habits.

equivocate (ih-KWIV-oh-kayt), verb
To intentionally use language that may deceive or be open to more than one interpretation
She knew she could no longer trust him when he began to equivocate instead of giving her straight answers.

eradicate (ih-RAD-ih-kayt), verb
To destroy, often at the very core of something; to eliminate completely
The president swore to eradicate illiteracy but his programs and ideas were unrealistic.

errant (AYR-unt), adjective
Moving away or straying from what is expected or considered the norm
Her errant behavior might have made her popular with other students but it got her in trouble with her teachers and the principal.

erratic (ih-RA-tik), adjective
Uneven; having no set or fixed course, either in direction or behavior
The man's erratic driving caused the police to pull him over because they suspected he was driving under the influence.

erroneous (ir-ROHN-ee-us), adjective
Incorrect or mistaken; full of errors
The results of the test were erroneous because the sample was tainted.

erudite (AYR-oo-dyt), adjective
Having great knowledge and intelligence; well spoken and knowledgeable
The university prided itself on having well-rounded, erudite graduates.

eschew (es-CHOO), verb
To deliberately avoid using; to reject the use of
After the war, the veteran spoke on the importance of eschewing violence.

espy (ih-SPY), verb
To notice; catch sight of; most commonly used in poetry
Romeo waited after the ball, hoping to espy Juliet in her window.

eulogy (yoo-LEH-gee), noun
A speech praising another person, traditionally one who has just died
The eulogy given at my father's funeral by his favorite student made us laugh and cry at the same time.

euphemism (YOO-fem-iz-um), noun
A mild, inoffensive term for something that might be considered rude, inappropriate, or vulgar
Many people prefer to use the euphemism "the little girls' room" instead of asking for the restroom or bathroom.

euphonious (YOO-fon-ee-us), adjective
Pleasing to the ear; nice to listen to
The sound of birds singing was particularly euphonious after the long, cold winter.

evince (ih-VINS), verb

To show clearly; to reveal; to put out in the open

Often, a society's mercy or lack thereof is evinced in the condition of its prisoners and how it treats its convicts.

evoke (EE-vohk), verb

To call or bring forth; to bring to mind or remind

The young politician's energy and demeanor evoked memories of John F. Kennedy and his campaign.

exalt (ig-ZAHLT), verb

To praise someone or something; to hold someone or something in high regard

Americans tend to exalt sports players and disregard teachers, nurses, and other important professionals.

exasperation (ig-zas-pur-RAY-shun), noun

Intense annoyance or irritation

His mother's exasperation was only intensified when he admitted not only was his homework not done, but he hadn't started on a major report that was due the next day.

excerpt (EK-surpt), noun

A short section taken from a larger piece of work, such as a movie, book, or other written work

The excerpt she read in the magazine was so engaging that she rushed out to buy the book.

execute (EKS-ih-kyoot), verb

To carry out or perform an action or deed

The gymnast was confident she could execute the routine flawlessly even under the pressure of competition.

exemplary (ek-ZEM-pla-ree), adjective

Close enough to ideal to serve as a model for others

At school, her behavior and attendance were exemplary, so no one suspected she was a wild child on the weekends.

exemplify (ek-ZEM-pleh-fiy), verb
To be or serve as an example
   The application required three writing samples that exemplified the students' writing styles.

exhaustive (eks-ZOH-stiv), adjective
Practically complete; including nearly all elements or aspects; thorough
   The editors' exhaustive research unearthed several little-known facts about the late senator.

exhilarating (ek-ZIL-er-ay-ting), adjective
Invigorating; happy, rejuvenating, and energetic
   The fast roller coaster was even more exhilarating than the riders had expected.

exigent (EG-sih-jent), adjective
Demanding immediate attention, usually referring to an emergency or dangerous situation
   Knowing basic first aid is essential in order to be helpful during an exigent situation.

exorbitant (eg-ZOR-bih-tant), adjective
Unreasonably high, generally refers to prices or financial cost
   During the gas shortage, the government froze prices so that no one could charge exorbitant prices for gasoline.

expatiate (eks-PAY-shee-ayt), verb
To be long-winded; to speak or write at length on a topic
   The old man tended to expatiate in answer to very simple questions.

expedient (ek-SPEE-dee-yent), adjective
Practical as a way to meet one's own needs; serving one's own self-interest
   It was expedient for her to do her chores without complaint since she wanted her mother's permission to go the party that night.

expedite (egs-PEH-diyt), verb
To make something happen faster than usual; to rush or hurry
   In order to get the package across the country in time for Christmas, the store had to expedite the shipment.

expiate (EK-spee-ayt), verb
To right a wrong; to make up for an intentional error; to cancel out
   She volunteered at the store hoping it would expiate her guilt at having shoplifted there.

explicate (EKS-plih-kayt), verb
To analyze an idea or written work in order to understand it clearly
   The assignment was to present and then explicate one of Shakespeare's sonnets so the class could understand the strange-sounding language more easily.

explicit (ek-SPLIH-siht), adjective
Clearly and with no room for interpretation; obvious; with nothing hidden
   Even with explicit directions to the airport, he still got lost on the way.

exploit (eks-PLOYT), verb or (EKS-ployt), noun
To use, often unethically or immorally, toward one's own ends (verb) or a brave, adventurous deed (noun)
   Child labor laws were enacted to prevent businesses from being able to exploit young children.
   Regardless of if they are fact or fiction, Robin Hood's exploits have entertained people for generations.

expostulate (eks-POS-choo-layt), verb
To express strong disagreement with the goal of changing another person's mind or attitude
   Most activists prefer to expostulate with the other side rather than resort to violence.

expropriate (eks-PRO-pree-ayt), verb

To take away from the rightful owner, usually an action performed by a government

Generally speaking, it is illegal for the government to simply expropriate property without offering its owners a fair market value.

extant (EKS-tent) or (eks-TENT), adjective

Still in existence; not lost or destroyed, usually refers to a document

Extant historical documents are important because they offer a glimpse into a former way of life.

extemporaneous (ek-stemp-ohr-RAY-nee-uhs), adjective

Performed or spoken with little or no preparation; done without notes

The motivational speaker was so good at her job that most people didn't realize her speeches were extemporaneous.

extenuating (ek-STEN-yoo-ay-ting), adjective

Something that lessens the seriousness or guilt of something else

Although she was late to her daughter's graduation, everyone understood there were extenuating circumstances once she explained the overflowing toilet.

extinct (ek-STINKT), adjective

No longer living or active

Geologists thought the volcano was extinct until it erupted, surprising everyone.

extinguish (ek-STING-gwish), verb

To put out; to put an end to

When the runner fell during the trials, his hopes for a gold medal were extinguished before he ever made it to the Olympics.

extirpate (EK-stuhr-payt), verb

To destroy at the core; to tear out from the roots

After the attacks on the World Trade Center, the United States stated it would extirpate terrorists and terrorism wherever they were hiding.

F

extol (ek-STOHL), verb

To praise greatly

The realtor extolled the benefits of living in the neighborhood to the point it sounded like heaven on earth.

extort (ek-STORT), verb

To obtain by threat or intimidation

The gang used the threat of violence to extort a "protection fee" from the local businesses.

extraneous (ek-STRAY-nee-us), adjective

Extra; not essential; not pertaining to the central topic

He knew the paragraph describing the farm itself was extraneous to his report on George Washington but he needed to make the report longer.

extricate (ek-STRIH-kayt), verb

To free from an entanglement or difficulty, may be physical or theoretical

She knew she had to extricate herself from the in-fighting at the office but she didn't know how to do so without risking her job.

exuberance (eg-ZOO-buhr-ans), noun

Joyous, unbridled enthusiasm

Seeing the children's exuberance when they finally arrived at the amusement park made the planning and expense worthwhile.

facetious (fuh-SEE-shus), adjective

Treating serious issues in a humorous manner; lighthearted in a way that is not always appropriate

The employees of the funeral home made facetious jokes when they were alone in order to stay detached from their work.

facile (FA-sihl), adjective

Easy to accomplish, often superficial and disregarding of the full issue

The facile solution presented by the school board disregarded the complex issues the principal dealt with on a day-to-day basis.

F

facilitate (fuh-SIL-ih-tayt), verb
To bring about; to make something easier to happen
The union's acceptance of the contract facilitated a quick resolution to the negotiations.

factious (FAK-shus), adjective
Produced by dissatisfaction within a larger group; internal strife or dissatisfaction
The complaints of the three members created a factious feeling among the entire board.

fallacious (fuhl-AY-shus), adjective
Based on something misunderstood or incorrect
She held the fallacious belief that Texas was the largest state in the country.

fallacy (FAHL-uh-see), noun
Something that is untrue, usually believed due to false logic or bad information
It is a fallacy that most states make it financially appealing to be on welfare, although it is a commonly held opinion.

fallow (FAHL-oo), adjective
Prepared for planting but left unsown in order to give the earth time to rejuvenate; inactive
The farmer left his southern fields fallow hoping to get a healthier crop in the freshened soil next season.

falter (FAHL-ter), verb
To hesitate or be unsteady, usually from fear; to lose courage and be unable to act
She felt her courage falter as they passed her the microphone but managed to give her opinion to the crowd anyway.

fanaticism (fa-NAT-ih-sizm), noun
Extreme, often irrational belief in something, characterized by criticism of differing viewpoints
Religious fanaticism exists in every country and religion in the world.

fathom (FA-thum), verb

To understand on a deep level; to truly comprehend

By his early twenties, the man finally realized he would never truly fathom the way women thought.

fawn (FAWN), verb

To flatter in a subservient manner in order to gain favor; may include putting oneself down in order to build the other person up

When he first won the award he enjoyed having everyone fawn over him but it rapidly became annoying and he longed for his old, down-to-earth friends.

Don't I Know That Word?

Sometimes a word you know may be used in an unfamiliar way. You may be unaware of its other definitions. Fawn (FAWN) is probably one of those words. You know that a fawn is a baby deer. That is its most common definition. However, it is also verb meaning to suck up to someone. Remember, even if you think you know the word, check the definition as well—just in case.

---

feasible (FEE-zih-bul), adjective

Possible to do or accomplish; easy to bring about

If she saved her baby-sitting money, spending a week on the beach was a feasible vacation.

feint (FAYNT), noun or verb

A false, misleading move intended to draw attention away from the real action or activity, usually used in sporting events (noun)

to make a misleading move with the intention of drawing away from the real action (verb)

The goalie had expected a feint on the penalty kick so was able to block the ball when it indeed came to her weak side instead.

The boxer had studied his opponent so he was ready when the other man tried to feint with his left and attack with his right.

fell (FEHL), verb

To cut or knock down; to topple

The hurricane felled trees and ripped roofs from houses but no lives were lost.

felon (FEHL-un), noun

A person who has committed a serious crime

The residents of the town locked their doors and windows until the escaped felon had been recaptured.

ferocity (fur-AH-sih-tee), noun

The state of being fierce or violent

The lion's ferocity was more intimidating in the wild than it had been at the zoo.

fervent (FUHR-vent), adjective

Having great emotion or passion; caring a great deal

The mother's fervent pleas for an organ donor moved everyone who heard them.

Similar but Not the Same

Two words with similar definitions may seem identical, but they are not used in exactly the same way. Fervent (FUHR-vent) and fervid (FUR-vid) are two of these words. The word fervent can be used to encompass a wide range of emotions. A person can be fervent in her anger, her joy, her grief, or her support—any number of strong emotions. Fervid, however, implies feeling a positive emotion. Fervid means enthusiastic, overjoyed, or another extreme sense of happiness.

fervid (FUR-vid), adjective

Intensely enthusiastic; wildly supportive or excited

The fervid crowd broke through the fence and stormed the field when the team won in the last seconds of the game.

fervor (FUR-vuhr), noun
Intense and passionate emotion
The fervor in Boston when the Red Sox finally won the World Series cannot be understood if you weren't there to experience it.

fidelity (fih-DEL-ih-tee), noun
Faithfulness and loyalty, expressed by continued support
She showed her fidelity to her alma mater with a generous check every year.

filibuster (FIL-eh-buhs-ter), noun
Delaying tactics, usually the making of long speeches, used in the legislature to postpone or prevent action being taken
The senator was three hours into the filibuster and showed no signs of yielding the floor to let the vote take place.

finesse (fin-ESS), noun
Refinement and delicacy; grace and skill
It took all the finesse the building manager had to juggle the needs and egos of all the artists performing at the benefit concert.

fitful (FIT-ful), adjective
Irregular; broken up; not steady
Her sleep was always fitful during exams because she was so stressed about the tests.

flagrant (FLAY-grehnt), adjective
Obviously bad or wrong; conspicuously offensive
Some people consider the verdict in the O.J. Simpson trial a flagrant miscarriage of justice while others consider it proof the criminal justice system works.

flamboyant (flam-BOI-ant), adjective
Elaborate; highly energetic; tending to draw attention
His eccentric aunt's house was as flamboyant as she was.

F

flippant (FLIP-uhnt), adjective
Disrespectful but often humorous; not showing seriousness
The young woman's flippant remark in response to his offer hurt him deeply but he refused to show it.

florid (FLOH-rid), adjective
Flushed with color, usually reddish; ruddy
His florid complexion made his mother realize he hadn't just been studying with his tutor.

flout (FLOWT), verb
To openly disregard or show contempt for
She dyed her hair purple as a safe way to flout the school's dress code.

fluidly (FLOO-id-lee), adverb
In a graceful, flowing way
The large cat moved fluidly through the grass as it stalked its prey.

foment (foh-MENT), verb
To incite or instigate; to stir up, usually to action
The speakers fomented the crowd, turning a peaceful gathering into a violent riot.

foolhardy (fool-HARD-ee), adjective
Rash; uncaring of the consequences; daring in an irresponsible way
His leap from the balcony into the pool was easily the most foolhardy thing any of the students did while on spring break.

foppish (FOHP-ish), adjective
Overly concerned with looks, style, and mannerism
Underneath the Scarlet Pimpernel's foppish exterior was a brave and daring man.

forbearance (for-BAYR-ens), noun
Patience and self-control, especially when faced with an annoyance
I was grateful to my tutor for treating me with such forbearance while I struggled to understand calculus.

forfeit (FOR-fit), verb or noun
To surrender or give up (verb) or something that is surrendered or given up, usually in payment (noun)

When the opposing team had to forfeit, our school felt cheated out of a good game.

The courts ruled that the forfeit of the farmer's land would be due the first day of the next month.

forgery (FOR-juh-ree), noun
Something that is a fake, made with the intention of presenting it as authentic

The Picasso forgery was so well made that even experts couldn't recognize it as fake just by looking at it.

forswear (for-SWAYR), verb
To deny, renounce, or agree to give up, usually in a formal setting such as under oath or before God

In order to save her life, Katherine Parr had to forswear that she was not Protestant but had only studied the teachings in order to better debate King Henry VIII.

fortuitous (for-TYOO-ih-tus), adjective
Occurring by lucky chance or happening; unexpected and unplanned but good

It was fortuitous that they were both walking in the park at the same time or they might never have met in a city the size of Houston.

fragile (FRAH-jul), adjective
Easily broken or destroyed; flimsy

She didn't allow the children to carry the china because it was fragile and they were clumsy.

frantic (FRAN-tik), adjective
Overcome with fear, anxiety, or another negative emotion

The young woman became frantic when her computer crashed with the only copy of her thesis on it.

frivolous (FRIV-uh-lus), adjective
Carefree; having no serious purpose
The ceramic purple and blue giraffe might have been a frivolous purchase but it made her very happy, so it was worth the money.

frugality (FROO-gal-ih-tee), noun
The ability to spend very little money; the ability to save without wasting much
He decided it was better to learn frugality than have to ask his parents for money again.

fugacious (fyoo-GAY-shus), adjective
Passing away quickly; fleeting; short lived
Between the heat in September and the snow in early November, autumn seemed even more fugacious than usual this year.

fulminate (fool-mih-NAYT), verb
To express violent disapproval; to protest vehemently
The murder of the little girl caused the mayor to fulminate against street crime at every opportunity.

fulsome (FOOL-sum), adjective
Excessive and insincere, used to define flattery or praise
His obviously fulsome praise of his boss backfired when he didn't get the promotion because he was such a brownnoser.

furtive (FUR-tiv), adjective
Hidden due to guilt or the belief that being seen or known would cause trouble
Although happily married himself, he couldn't help but steal furtive glances at his friend's beautiful wife.

gainsay (GAYN-say), verb
To deny, contradict, or state something is false
She wanted to gainsay the accusations against her friend but couldn't because she knew they were true.

gamut (GAA-mut), noun
The whole or complete range of something
>*The audience experienced the gamut of emotions, from grief and rage to love and elation, right along with the actors on stage.*

germane (jer-MAYN), adjective
Relevant to the topic at hand; pertinent to what is being discussed
>*Students' participation in class is germane when considering their grades.*

gesticulate (jes-TIK-yoo-layt), verb
To use gestures while speaking, especially for emphasis
>*The more passionate she was about a topic, the more she gesticulated when discussing it.*

glacial (GLAY-shul), adjective
Extremely cold, either in demeanor, manner, or temperature
>*The glacial stare she sent him when he walked in the room made it clear to the rest of us their relationship had ended badly.*

glib (GLIHB), adjective
Natural to the point of being off-handed; without much depth, shallow
>*The girl's glib response when questioned about her homework concerned her father because he knew she hadn't started on the report.*

glimmer (GLIHM-ehr), noun
An intermittent flicker of light; or a faint glimpse
>*The glimmer of the Christmas tree lights and the glow of the fire made the room cozy and romantic.*
>*The young man had a glimmer of hope that she might be interested in him when she gave him her phone number.*

glutton (GLUT-un), noun
A person who eats an enormous amount; or a person who can withstand or even longs for a large amount of something
>*All-you-can-eat buffets tend to be heaven for gluttons.*
>*When he started dating yet another self-centered woman, his friends started wondering if he was a glutton for punishment.*

gossamer (GOS-ih-mer), noun
Something light, flimsy, and delicate, often referring to very delicate material
At the sight of the flowers on her desk, her bad mood dissolved like gossamer.

G

gourmand (gor-MAND), noun
A person who loves good food
The newspaper's food critic was well-suited to the job because she was such a gourmand.

grandiloquence (grand-EHL-ih-kwens), noun
A pompous and pretentious way of speaking; a manner of talking that suggests the speaker is trying too hard to impress
The speaker's grandiloquence impressed some but merely put off others.

gratify (GRA-tih-fiy), verb
To please or satisfy
The teacher was always gratified when her students were accepted into college.

gratuitous (grah-TOO-ih-tus), adjective
Unnecessary and uncalled for; unwanted; extra or unneeded
Sadly, movie makers have learned that gratuitous sex and violence sells tickets.

Don't I Know That Word?
Words often have a second (or third) meaning that is less common than its best-known definition. Gravity (gra-VUH-tee) is one of those words. You know that gravity is the force that keeps everything on the planet from floating off the earth. However, it also means seriousness or importance.

gravity (gra-VUH-tee), adjective
Seriousness, great importance
The drunken teens' parents called the police in order to help reinforce the gravity of the situation.

grievous (GREE-vus), adjective
Devastating; causing severe pain, either emotional or physical
> *Only time will tell if the city will ever recover from the grievous loss caused by the hurricane that struck this year.*

gullible (GUL-uh-bul), adjective
Easily made to believe something false; easy to fool
> *Con artists count on people being gullible enough to believe their scams.*

halcyon (HAL-see-yon), adjective
Idyllic; peaceful and calm; often used when describing a particular time from the past
> *Many people look back on the summers of their childhoods and consider them halcyon days, forgetting that those same days were often boring at the time.*

hamper (HAM-per), verb
To hinder or prevent free movement; to hold back, literally or figuratively
> *Her friends told her that the umbrella would only hamper her on the hike but she insisted on taking it anyway.*

Don't I Know That Word?

Even if you think you know a word, you may find it used in an unfamiliar context. Check the definition—it may have a second meaning you were unaware of. Hamper (HAM-per) may be one of those words. You know that a hamper is a container, usually where you throw your dirty laundry. That is its most common definition. But it is also verb that means to hold back or make difficult.

---

harangue (hu-RANG), noun
A long, critical speech or lecture
> *The young man refused to return his sister's phone call because he knew it would just be another hour-long harangue about what a bad brother he was.*

H

hardy (HAR-dee), adjective
Capable of living in just about any condition
Aloe plants are hardy, which makes them ideal for city apartments that don't get much light or fresh air.

haughtiness (HAW-tee-ness), noun
Arrogance; superiority; condescending pride
The haughtiness of the contestant lost her points in the personality category.

headlong (HED-long), adjective
Rashly and without much thought; or headfirst
The young couple rushed headlong into marriage without considering that they were making a lifetime commitment at only eighteen years old.
She fell headlong down the stairs but only received a few bruises.

hedonist (HEED-on-ist), noun
A person who believes only in the pursuit of pleasure
The socialite had a reputation as a hedonist only because she kept her numerous charitable activities private.

hegemony (heh-JOHM-eh-nee), noun
Leadership or dominance, usually in regards to government or the relationship between nations
When a nation is very wealthy and powerful, it is important that it not abuse its state of hegemony on the global stage.

heinous (HAY-nus), adjective
Particularly vicious or offensive on a societal level, not just a personal one
The police released few details to the public due to the heinous nature of the crime.

heresy (HAYR-ih-see), noun
A belief or statement that goes against religious doctrine
In ancient times, heresy was a crime punished by torture and execution.

heretical (huh-RHET-ih-cul), adjective
Characterized by beliefs that differ from accepted religious beliefs, generally holds a negative connotation
　　Strict followers of a religion tend to find other faiths heretical and in need of saving and redemption.

heterogeneous (het-tuh-ROH-jee-nus), adjective
Diverse; consisting of many, dissimilar parts
　　She loved living in the city partly because of its heterogeneous population and diverse neighborhoods.

hirsute (hur-SOOT), adjective
Hairy, covered in hair
　　Hirsute caterpillars didn't bother him but bare, slimy worms made him cringe.

homogeneous (HO-mah-jee-nus), adjective
Similar; consisting of many, similar parts
　　With the Internet, chat rooms, and easier international communication, few people have a homogeneous social circle any longer.

hoodwink (HUHD-wink), verb
To trick or deceive; to fool; to put one over on
　　Her attempts to hoodwink her parents failed when they discovered she had sneaked out after midnight.

hospitable (hahs-PIT-a-bul), adjective
Friendly and welcoming; or having an open mind; being willing to hear new ideas
　　The innkeepers had to be hospitable, even when they were having bad days themselves.
　　The principal was hospitable to suggestions from the seniors regarding a new venue for the prom.

hubris (HYOO-bris), noun
Arrogant or overwhelming pride
　　In many Greek myths, mortals' hubris causes them to think they can successfully challenge the gods, but they always lose in the end.

hypocrisy (hih-POK-ruh-see), noun
The act of saying one thing and doing another; the practice of stating a certain belief and then acting differently from that belief
When a smoker discourages someone from lighting up, it is not hypocrisy but an earnest desire to prevent someone from making the same mistake the smoker made.

hypocritical (hip-ih-KRIT-ih-kul), adjective
To express feelings one doesn't really have or feel; to behave in a way one has criticized
The young woman's friends ignored her hypocritical comments about flirting because they knew she behaved the same way when they weren't around.

What I Meant to Say Was . . .

Don't get tripped up by words that look or sound almost identical! Hypocritical (hip-ih-KRIT-ih-kul) and hypothetical (hiy-po-THET-ih-kul) can easily be confused, especially when you are reading quickly. To be hypocritical is to be two-faced and behave in ways that you have condemned. If something is hypothetical, it is based on an assumption or theory.

---

hypothetical (hiy-po-THET-ih-kul), adjective
Based on a supposition; not real
It is easier to make difficult decisions in hypothetical situations because there are no real consequences.

idiosyncrasy (id-dee-oh-SINK-ra-see), noun
A characteristic specific to a certain person; a quirk
One of her idiosyncrasies was that she liked to burn candles while she worked at her desk.

idolatrous (iy-DAHL-eh-trus), adjective
Adoring a person or thing to the level of worship
Tabloid magazines helped create the idolatrous feelings society tends to have toward movie and television stars.

ignoble (ig-NOH-bul), adjective
Common, ordinary, or plain; not overly honorable or impressive
People were shocked to see the candidate doing something as ignoble as shopping at the mall.

illicit (ih-LIS-it), adjective
Forbidden or illegal; prohibited; immoral or improper
The teacher knew the paper had been obtained through illicit means because the same one had been turned in the previous year by another student.

illusory (ih-LOO-suh-ree), adjective
Not real; based on an illusion or wish; based in fantasy rather than fact
The safety the women had felt on campus was proven to be illusory when a young woman was attacked.

imbroglio (im-BROHL-yoh), noun
A complicated, entangled, confusing, and often embarrassing situation
The Iran-Contra imbroglio will always be important in the study of the politics of the late 1980s.

imbue (im-BYOO), verb
Influence deeply, pervade; inspired by; often used with "with" or "by"
Her discussions were imbued with ideas first taught by the great philosophers.

immaculate (ih-MAH-kyoo-leht), adjective
Perfectly clean, spotless; free from stain or marking
While he hadn't expected his son's dorm room to be immaculate, he was still shocked at how messy it was.

imminent (ih-MIH-nent), adjective
About to happen; immediate; due to occur at any moment
The crowd knew the president's arrival was imminent when the Secret Service started clearing everyone from the path.

immutable (ih-MYOO-tah-bul), adjective
Set and stable; not subject to change
   It is an immutable fact that teenagers will find some way to rebel against their parents and societal expectations.

impair (im-PAYR), verb
To weaken or diminish; to make less effective
   Her cold medication left her groggy and impaired her ability to drive to the doctor's office, so her friend drove her instead.

impassive (im-PAS-iv), adjective
Showing no emotion; having no particular expression
   The principal stayed impassive even though he wanted to laugh during the young man's outlandish explanation.

impeccable (im-PEK-uh-bul), adjective
Meeting the highest standards; perfect
   Her outfits were always so impeccable that she looked like she could have stepped out of a fashion magazine.

impecunious (im-peh-KYOO-nee-us), adjective
Having little money; poor
   Although his family was in an impecunious situation after the layoffs, he still managed to get birthday presents for his children.

impede (im-PEED), noun
To delay or prevent something from continuing
   The United Nations refused to let the threat of violence impede the elections in the small country.

imperative (im-PAYR-ih-tiv), adjective
Absolutely necessary; required; urgent
   She wore a medical alert bracelet because it was imperative that doctors know she was allergic to penicillin in the case of a medical emergency.

imperturbable (im-per-TUR-bih-bul), adjective
Calm and collected at all times; unable to be shocked or disturbed
    Part of what made him an effective teacher was his ability to make his students believe he was truly imperturbable, regardless of what stunts they pulled.

impervious (im-PER-vee-us), adjective
Impossible to affect; immune to reaction
    Having grown up in New England, she was impervious to southern winters.

impetus (IHM-puh-tus), noun
The motivation or stimulus behind movement or change
    The sleeveless bridesmaid's dress was the impetus she needed to lose the twenty pounds that had been plaguing her.

impiety (ihm-PIY-ih-tee), noun
Lack of reverence or respect, especially toward God
    Although teenagers often speak with impiety, studies show that their faith is strong and religion is important to many of them.

implacable (ihm-PLAHK-ih-bul), adjective
Impossible or unable to appease; or relentless and unstoppable
    The professor had a reputation for being implacable because of her high and uncompromising standards.
    Once the dam was breeched, the river was implacable on its path toward the town.

implausible (ihm-PLOH-zih-bul), adjective
Unbelievable; not seeming reasonable or true
    As the school year went on, her excuses for not doing her work became more and more implausible.

implement (IHM-pleh-ment), noun or verb
A tool used for work; a way to achieve a goal (noun) or to put into practice or action, generally plans or ideas (verb)
    A prepared worker always has the right implement for each job.
    The boss of the organization decided to implement new ideas in order to keep the company state of the art.

implicate (IHM-plih-kayt), verb

To show a close connection between two things, usually in an incriminating, criminal, or negative way

She took the proof of illegal hazing to the school dean even though she knew doing so would implicate her own sorority.

implicit (im-PLIH-sit), adjective

Implied though not stated directly; or inherent; essentially part of something even if not obvious; or without doubt; having no questions or reservations

The threat implicit in dealing with Al Capone was one every person in Chicago understood during Prohibition.

When someone joins the military just to pay for college, he needs to understand the implicit risk of being sent to war instead.

Children's implicit faith in Santa Claus is heartwarming and helps remind adults of simpler times.

importunate (ihm-POR-cheh-nant), adjective

Persistent to the point of being annoying

His niece was importunate in her requests for specific and elaborate birthday presents.

importune (ihm-por-TOON), verb

To frequently and repeatedly ask, urge, or request something of another person, usually implies being annoying

She considered repeating her request for a raise but didn't want to importune her boss with the issue.

impregnable (im-PREG-nuh-bul), adjective

Impossible to be attacked or brought down, referring to a structure, idea, or argument

Although she made her case badly, the core facts were truly impregnable so she won the debate in spite of her poor performance.

impromptu (ihm-promp-TOO), adjective

Spur of the moment; happening without a plan, purpose, or rehearsal

The impromptu party that developed on his floor canceled out the plans for studying he had made earlier in the week.

improvident (ihm-PRAHV-ih-dent), adjective
Showing little or no forethought or planning; not thinking of the future
   Her shopping spree was improvident in light of her tuition bill being due at the end of the month.

impudence (IM-pyeh-dens), noun
Uncaringly disrespectful; offensively bold or forthright
   The young man's impudence was an indication that his mother had lost control over his behavior.

impunity (im-PYOO-nih-tee), noun
Exempt from punishment; free from consequence
   She had always acted with impunity because of her father's standing in the community, so getting into trouble at college was a rude awakening for her.

impute (ihm-PYOOT), verb
To assign or attribute, usually fault, blame, or responsibility, to another
   Children often try to impute bad behaviors to imaginary friends.

inadvertently (IN-ad-ver-tant-lee), adverb
Accidentally; unintentionally; caused by being unintentionally negligent
   He immediately regretted the offhanded comment that had inadvertently caused his friend so much pain.

inane (in-NAYN), adjective
Without substance; silly; pointless
   The sitcom's inane humor and shallow characters appealed to some people but not enough to keep it on the air.

inchoate (in-KOH-ayt), adjective
New enough to not be fully formed or established; at an early stage
   It is unfair to judge an inchoate democracy by the same standards the United States can manage with ease.

incidental (IN-sih-dent-uhl), adjective
Happening along with but secondary to the major event; minor and less significant
The movie being filmed on site became incidental to the Red Sox winning the World Series.

incisive (in-SIY-sihv), adjective
Accurate, sharp, and penetrating, in regards to a mind, concept, or theory
The professor really looked forward to his senior classes because of his students' incisive, thought-provoking comments on world politics.

incite (in-SIYT), verb
To stir up or provoke; to encourage or urge on, usually violent behavior or dissension
Tensions were so high during the trial that the police presence actually incited the crowds to violence rather than keeping the peace.

Watch Out!

It's often possible to change the parts of speech of a word simply by adding a suffix. But similar looking words are not always related. Although incisive and incite appear to be different forms of the same word, they really are not. Incisive (in-SIY-sihv) means penetrating. To incite (in-SIYT) means to stir up or provoke. Be careful not to confuse the two.

inclusive (in-KLOO-sihv), adjective
Including all aspects; comprehensive; including the limits at the extremes
Some sociologists believe that unless the two major political parties find a way to be more inclusive, it is just a matter of time before a third-party candidate wins a major election.
The assignment was to work problems one through twenty-five, inclusive, but many students stopped at number twenty-four.

incompatible (in-kohm-PAT-ih-bul), adjective
Unable to exist at the same time; incapable of living or associating in harmony
Living in Dallas, Texas, tends to be incompatible with being a Washington Redskins fan.

incongruous (in-KOHN-groo-uhs), adjective
Out of place or inappropriate; deeply unexpected; not in line with what is expected or appropriate

The fast food restaurant was incongruous with the quaint surroundings of the New England village.

inconsequential (in-KOHN-sih-kwen-shul), adjective
Unimportant; trivial

In light of her overall GPA, the one B+ was inconsequential to the universities that were courting her.

incorrigible (in-KOHR-ih-jeh-bul), adjective
Incapable of being reformed, corrected, or improved; used when describing a person or behavior

When the public school deemed the young woman incorrigible, her parents chose to send her to private school rather than risk her getting involved with gang activity during her suspension.

incredulity (in-kreh-DYOO-lih-tee), noun
The state of disbelief, doubt regarding truth; the state of being unwilling or unable to believe

He didn't blame anyone for having a sense of incredulity when he passed science since he had struggled with the subject all year.

indelible (in-DEHL-ih-bul), adjective
Impossible to erase, mark out, remove, or forget

The girl's first meeting of Mickey Mouse was an indelible memory she secretly carried with her throughout her life.

indict (in-DIYT), verb
To charge or accuse of wrongdoing, often a crime but not necessarily

Instead of just presenting the award as planned, the actor took a moment at the podium to indict the government for its handling of the war.

indifferent (in-DIHF-her-ehnt), adjective
Having no feelings one way or another; uncaring or unconcerned
She realized she was truly over her ex-boyfriend when she learned he was dating someone else and she was actually indifferent to the fact.

indigenous (in-DIJ-ih-nus), adjective
Naturally occurring in a specific place; native
Many plants indigenous to the rain forests cannot be found anywhere else on the planet.

indigent (IN-deh-jent), adjective
Impoverished; in need or wanting; poor
Many people find great satisfaction in helping indigent families during the holidays.

indiscriminate (in-dis-KRIM-ih-nat), adjective
Happening randomly, without plan or logic; seemingly confused or without a specific pattern
Her indiscriminate taste in music made it difficult to know if she would like a particular band or not.

indistinct (in-dih-STINKT), adjective
Unclear, foggy, or hazy; not well defined, referring to a thought, concept, or physical entity
The directions were vague, leaving them only the most indistinct idea of how to get to the party.

indolence (IN-dul-ens), noun
Laziness; the state of avoiding work or exertion
He stopped working out because of a muscle injury, but sheer indolence kept him from returning to it once he was healed.

indomitable (in-DOM-ih-tuh-bul), adjective
Impossible to beat, conquer, or break down; unable to be subdued
Most cancer survivors possessed an indomitable will to live during their treatment in spite of their diagnosis or prognosis.

induce (in-DOOS), verb
To cause or bring about; to convince or persuade someone to take an action
He helped her with her homework secretly hoping to induce her to break up with her boyfriend.

indulgent (in-DUL-jent), adjective
Being overly lenient; not being able to say no to someone's wishes or wants
People disagree about how indulgent parents can be with their children before the children become spoiled.

ineffable (in-EHF-ah-bul), adjective
Unable to be described in words, usually because something is so great, glorious, or overwhelming
Tourists are often made speechless by the ineffable beauty of the Grand Canyon at first sight.

ineluctable (in-uh-LUK-tuh-bul), adjective
Unavoidable and inescapable; unable to turn back or stop
Romeo and Juliet's fate and ineluctable heartbreak were sealed from the moment they fell in love.

inept (in-EPT), adjective
Having little or no skill, sense, or judgment; incompetent
Superman hid his abilities behind the inept persona of Clark Kent.

inert (in-ERT), adjective
Without the ability or desire to move; still and lethargic; showing or having no reaction
After finals week, the students sat inert in front of the television for the whole day.

inevitable (in-EHV-ih-tah-bul), adjective
Unable to be stopped, unavoidable; certain to occur
The new father knew it was inevitable that his baby girl would grow up so he enjoyed every moment of her childhood.

infelicitous (in-feh-LIS-ih-tuhs), adjective
Inappropriate, not thought out, or poorly chosen
   They realized just how infelicitous it had been to toilet paper the principal's yard when she drove up and caught them in the act.

infuse (in-FYOOZ), verb
To fill up or permeate; to spread throughout
   As more decorations went up, the room became infused with the lights, colors, and sounds of the holidays.

ingénue (AHN-jzeh-nyoo), noun
An innocent young woman; often the role or character of an innocent young woman in a play
   The actress knew with her voluptuous figure and throaty laugh she was more suited to playing the sidekick than the ingénue.

ingenuous (in-JEN-yoo-uhs), adjective
Innocent, unworldly, and trusting; open to the point of being gullible; usually has a positive connotation rather than a negative one
   It was endearing to see how truly ingenuous the teenagers were the first time they saw New York City.

Similar but Not the Same

Many words are virtually synonymous—but this doesn't mean they are interchangeable. This is the case for inherent (in-HEYR-ent) and innate (ih-NAYT). Use the word inherent when you are describing an aspect of a thing, an activity, or an idea. An inherent aspect is one that cannot be completely removed from this thing, activity, or idea. Generally speaking, however, innate describes an aspect or a part of a person or other living creature. An innate aspect is one that is not learned but is with a person from birth, and therefore cannot be completely removed from that person.

---

inherent (in-HEYR-ent), adjective
A natural and vital part of something else; an essential part of a larger whole that cannot be removed
   The inherent risk in extreme sports is part of their allure for many participants.

inimical (ih-NIHM-ih-cul), adjective
Counterproductive; causing harm or the opposite of the desired effect
   His girlfriend's urgings that he attend the party were inimical to his studying for the test he had the next day.

innate (ih-NAYT), adjective
Existing from birth; natural and inborn; essentially a part of something; coming naturally, not learned
   His parents discovered he had an innate ear for music when he sat down at a piano and began to play when he was only five.

innocuous (ih-NAWK-yoo-uhs), adjective
Completely harmless to the point of being disregarded; tame; not offensive
   It took several bad relationships before she finally saw nice guys as being more than totally innocuous.

innovation (in-oh-VAY-shun), noun
A new creation, usually that moves a field forward in some way
   Scientists expect medical innovations to increase human life expectancies by many years.

inscrutable (in-SKROOT-uh-bul), adjective
Difficult or impossible to understand or know; incomprehensible; hard to get a handle on, as in a person, attitude, or concept
   The contestants tried to read the judges in order to guess the result, but their faces were inscrutable throughout the competition.

insensible (in-SENS-uh-bul), adjective
Too small to be noticed or to register; imperceptible; or temporarily unconscious or without feeling, usually due to external factors such as alcohol, violence, or extreme temperature; or unaware, insensitive to or indifferent; uncaring; unfeeling emotionally
   None of them noticed the insensible change in the light as the sun set until they realized they were sitting in the dark and had to turn on a light.
   The blow to the head knocked the boxer insensible for several minutes.
   She wasn't insensible toward her students' complaints but knew they needed the extra work if they were going to pass the test.

insinuate (in-SIN-yoo-ayt), verb
To hint, suggest, or subtly make known, generally regarding something negative; or to introduce oneself into a setting through crafty and somewhat unwelcome or negative means
Although his words seemed innocent enough, everyone knew he was trying to insinuate that the director was doing a poor job.
She was able to insinuate herself into the queen's inner circle through subtle bribery and indirect threats.

insipid (in-SIP-id), adjective
Unexciting; lacking in flavor, life, or vigor; boring and dull
After living in the city, she found life in a small town insipid and unbearable.

insolvent (in-SOL-vent), adjective
Unable to pay debts or what is owed; without money or assets
The president of the small company knew if they did not win a contract soon, the company would become insolvent and would have to close.

insouciant (in-SOO-see-aynt), adjective
Casual indifference or unconcerned; nonchalant
Although he tried to be insouciant about his acceptance to an Ivy League college, his friends knew he was very excited about it.

instigate (in-STIH-gayt), verb
To stir up or urge; to start, begin, or initiate
Even after years of marriage, they couldn't agree on which one of them instigated their first kiss.

insularity (IN-sul-ayr-ih-tee or INS-yoo-layr-ih-tee), noun
The state of being detached, either physically or emotionally; characterized by having little or no contact with others
In a world as intertwined as earth, no government can afford an attitude of complete insularity and expect its nation to thrive.

insuperable (in-SOO-per-ah-bul), adjective
Impossible to beat, overcome, or rise above, such as a challenge or obstacle
Stories of heroes facing insuperable odds and still succeeding have long been used to motivate individuals to achieve great things.

insurrection (in-suhr-REK-shun), noun
A violent uprising or revolt against a government or group in power
Many insurrections in East Germany were put down before the Berlin Wall finally fell in the latter part of the twentieth century.

integrity (in-TEG-rih-tee), noun
The state of having and living by a strong sense of morals and values; walking the walk as well as talking the talk; or the state of being complete and strong, without noticeable weaknesses or flaws, generally refers to a structure or concept
He enjoyed doing business with people who had a sense of integrity that was as strong as his own.
After the earthquake, the integrity of the bridge was called into question, so it was closed until tests could be performed and analyzed.

interim (IN-ter-ihm), noun or adjective
The time between the end of one event or period and the beginning of another (noun) or temporary, occurring between the end of one event and the beginning of another (adjective)
He knew he would be working very hard up until the end of the semester and would start working hard again once his job started in September, so he decided to relax during the interim.
The United Nations set up an interim government at the end of the hostilities until the country could hold its own elections.

intervene (in-tehr-VEEN), verb
To come between two things, often to prevent something from occurring
The camp counselor waited to intervene in the argument to see if the two boys could work it out between them.

intimidate (in-TIHM-ih-dayt), verb
To frighten or make nervous; to make someone afraid by using threats
Although she wasn't easily intimidated, the thought of meeting the president made her more than a little nervous.

intractable (in-TRAKT-ah-bul), adjective
Hard to manage, control, or handle; stubborn; resistant
The mother was intractable when it came to making compromises about her children's health and well-being.

intransigent (in-TRAN-zih-jent), adjective
Unwilling to change or alter; uncompromising; stubbornly refusing to be persuaded or changed
Once he had made up his mind, he was intransigent regardless of what new information might be presented to him.

intrepid (in-TREH-pid), adjective
Unusually courageous or bold; fearless; not able to be intimidated or frightened, may be used humorously or tongue in cheek
His intrepid approach to women had gained him a reputation as a lady's man.

introspection (in-troh-SPEK-shun), noun
The honest examination of one's own thoughts, feelings, motivations, and beliefs
It was only after much introspection that she could admit she wanted to be a doctor, not a teacher, as everyone had always expected.

intuitive (in-TOO-ih-tiv), adjective
Based on gut feeling, instinct, or emotion rather than fact and specific information; or easily understood; user friendly
Successful police officers often work with their intuitive feelings as well as the facts presented to them in order to solve a case.
The Web site was intuitive and therefore easy for users to navigate.

inundate (IN-un-dayt), verb

To overwhelm or flood; can be literal or figurative

Every year, colleges and universities are inundated with requests for information and applications.

inure (in-YOOR), verb

To become used to or accustomed to something, usually something very unpleasant, through repetition or constant exposure

Although visitors to the ranch noticed the smell, she had become inured to it after several weeks of working there.

invalid (IN-vuh-lihd), noun or (in-VAL-id), adjective

Someone who is disabled by sickness or injury, often used to describe a weak person who needs caretaking (noun) or not legitimate legally or factually; untrue; based on faulty logic or reasoning (adjective)

She refused to be called an invalid just because she was in a wheelchair after the accident.

Debates with him were often frustrating because he was unable to see that his arguments were generally invalid in light of the facts.

inveigh (in-VAY), verb

To write or speak out against something with great anger and passion; to be against an attitude, belief, or behavior in the strongest possible way; to condemn

South Africa was liberated from apartheid because brave men and women were willing to inveigh against the injustice inherent in the system.

inveigle (in-VAY-gul), verb

To gain or obtain something through flattery; to win over with sweet talk, often false or put on for the occasion

His friends were always amazed at how he was able to inveigle so many phone numbers from different women in one night.

invert (in-VERT), verb
To swap or reverse the order; or to turn inside out; or to turn upside down; or to turn inward

The young woman decided to invert two of the digits in her phone number to make sure he couldn't reach her later.

Everyone in the dorm pretended not to notice that her blouse was inverted when she came home from her date.

The young man inverted a cross that he wore around his neck because he knew it drove his parents crazy.

The clerk's foot was inverted, giving him a slightly pigeon-toed look.

inveterate (in-VEH-ter-uht), adjective
Long-standing, deep-rooted, and unlikely to change

Even though she was over eighty years old, she was still an inveterate flirt.

invidious (in-VIH-dee-us), adjective
Likely to make others angry, jealous, or envious; creating hostility among others; or containing or hinting at discrimination

He was so well liked that his election wasn't invidious, even to the people who were running against him.

Her comments about her lesbian roommate seemed innocent enough but were actually subtly invidious.

invincible (in-VIN-sih-bul), adjective
Incapable of being beaten, subdued, or overcome

The baseball team's invincible spirit took them into the playoffs when other, more skilled teams failed to get there.

iota (IY-oh-dah), noun
An insignificant amount; so small as to be imperceptible. Also the ninth letter of the Greek alphabet.

Her arguments for a later curfew didn't change her parents' opinion even an iota.

irascible (ih-RAS-ih-bul), adjective
Angry and mean; easily made upset or angry
> *The young children in the neighborhood avoided going near the irascible old man's house, but the older kids considered it a great challenge.*

Similar but Not the Same
Their definitions may seem identical, but that doesn't mean two words can be used exactly the same way. Irascible (ih-RAS-ih-bul) and irate (iy-RAYT) are two of these words. The word irascible describes someone's overall personality. Irate, however, just means a person is very angry at the moment about something specific. Be aware of the subtle differences between words that seem the same.

---

irate (iy-RAYT), adjective
Enraged; extremely angry; furious
> *The judge became irate at the continued outbursts in her courtroom.*

ire (IYR), noun
Fury; anger; wrath
> *By the time they were seniors, every student had learned not to bring on the ire of the principal.*

irksome (URK-sum), adjective
Annoying, irritating, and bothersome; tedious and boring to the point of annoyance
> *Although she loved teaching, she found grading papers irksome and monotonous.*

ironic (iy-RON-ik), adjective
The opposite of what is expected, in an emotionally moving, poignant way
> *He had been so outspoken against the war that it was ironic when he discovered joining the military was the only way he could pay for college.*

irreproachable (eer-ree-PROH-chah-bul), adjective
Beyond fault or criticism; perfect and without blemish
> *The press quickly learned the candidate's personal life was irreproachable so had to look for scandal elsewhere.*

itinerant (iy-TIN-er-ehnt), adjective
Characterized by moving from place to place, usually in order to perform one's job
Actors who join touring companies must accept and enjoy an itinerant way of life or else they quickly change professions.

itinerate (iy-TIN-er-ayt), verb
To move from one place to another, one town to another, usually to perform one's job
The salesman had to itinerate seven out of every eight weeks in order to meet his quota.

jocular (JAHK-yoo-lur), adjective
Good-natured, humorous; given to jokes; generally happy; funny and playful
The old man's jocular nature made him a favorite with all the children of the neighborhood, not just his own grandchildren.

jovial (JOH-vee-ahl), adjective
Joyful, happy, full of good cheer; friendly; sincerely warm emotionally
The party's success was based largely on the jovial hostess, who made everyone feel so welcome in her home.

Similar but Not the Same

Don't confuse words that have similar meanings. Jocular (JAHK-yoo-lur) and jovial (JOH-vee-ahl) are two of these words. The word jocular tends to describe someone who will actually make jokes or make people laugh as well as just be a happy, warm person. Jovial, however, does not carry the implication of jokes or humor.

jubilation (joo-bih-LAY-shun), noun
Extreme joy and happiness; nearly overwhelming elation; rejoicing
As reserved as the man usually was, he couldn't hide his jubilation at the news he was going to be a father.

K

judiciously (joo-DISH-us-lee), adverb
Marked by good sense; having sound judgment; using reason and logic to come to or behave in an appropriate way
    The company hired her full-time after they saw her handle the crisis judiciously and calmly.

junta (JUN-tuh or HUN-tuh), noun
A group, usually military, that takes control of the government by force in order to rule the country
    The weak government of the small island was easy prey for the general and his junta.

kinetic (kih-NEH-tik), adjective
Relating to or characterized by motion
    The toddler's kinetic activities quickly tired his babysitter but hardly seemed to slow him down at all.

kith (KIHTH), noun
Friends and close acquaintances; almost always used in the phrase kith and kin, meaning friends and family
    The young woman's kith and kin gathered from all over the country to see her receive the award from the President.

knobbly (NOB-blee), adjective
Having lumps or bumps that resemble knobs
    The fruit from the island was knobbly enough that some of the tourists couldn't figure out how to eat it until their guide showed them how to peel the rind by pulling one of the bumps.

kohl (KOL), noun
A black powder, used especially in Egypt and the Middle East, to darken and outline the eyes
    In ancient Egypt, both the male and female members of a royal family would use kohl around their eyes in order to enhance their looks.

kowtow (KOW-tow), verb

To act in a particularly subservient manner in hopes of gaining favor; to brownnose

The entire department was embarrassed watching the director kowtow to the CEO when she made her yearly visit of all the programs.

labyrinth (LAB-ih-rinth), noun

A complicated and difficult path that is very hard to find the way through; a maze; or anything that is overly complex, difficult to navigate

One of the most popular destinations for teenagers during Halloween was the haunted labyrinth the town set up each year.

When dealing with bureaucracies, finding one's way through the labyrinth of red tape can be a frustrating and time-consuming event.

lachrymose (LAK-ree-mohs), adjective

Crying, weeping, in tears; or sorrowful; prone to cause tears or crying

The news of the latest terrorist attack had most of the nation lachrymose.

Hoping to counter the lachrymose air, he told humorous stories about his friend at the funeral.

lackadaisical (lak-uh-DAY-zihk-uhl), adjective

Lacking care or energy; carelessly lazy; unconcernedly indifferent

Her parents were concerned that her lackadaisical approach to her schoolwork would prevent her from being accepted to the college of her choice.

lament (luh-MENT), verb or noun

To grieve or mourn, openly and often loudly; or to deeply regret; to feel great remorse (verb) or the feeling or expression of deep, heart-wrenching grief; or a work, such as a song or poem, expressing deep sadness, grief (noun)

Flowers and notes were left at the memorial by numerous fans lamenting the singer for years after his murder.

As she grew older, she often lamented the poor choices she had made as a teenager and young adult.

The lament that spread through the town the first few days after the hurricane was soon replaced by a desire to rebuild and move on with life.

The composer was known for his laments, so few people knew he could also write cheerful airs and waltzes.

lampoon (lahm-POON), noun or verb

A work that makes fun of a person, event, or situation in a joking, satirical manner (noun) or to tease or make fun of something; to satirize or mock jokingly (verb)

The sketch performed at orientation was a lampoon of college life, written to calm the freshmen's nerves about starting school.

He knew he was in trouble when the teacher he was lampooning caught him in the act.

Which Word?

Many words can be used as either a noun or a verb. Lampoon (lahm-POON) is one of them. The verb to lampoon means to make fun of something. The noun lampoon is the skit, joke, cartoon—or anything else—that is being used to make fun. In other words, the comedian can lampoon the politician in a lampoon.

---

lascivious (luh-SIHV-ee-us), adjective

Feeling or showing overt, inappropriate, and usually offensive lust or sexual desire

The lascivious looks she received at the bar made the group decide to get their drinks elsewhere.

lassitude (LAS-ih-tood), noun

The state of being overly tired, drained, or lacking energy; physically or mentally tired and worn out

A feeling of lassitude filled the locker room after the team's heartbreaking loss in overtime.

latent (LAY-tent), adjective

In existence but hidden or unknown; potential; undiscovered or undeveloped

It only took a few classes for her to realize she had a latent talent for interior decorating and design.

laudable (LAW-dih-bul), adjective
Deserving of praise; commendable; noteworthy
Although the quarterback's performance was laudable, it couldn't make up for the defense's poor showing.

laudatory (LAW-dih-toh-ree), adjective
Giving or expressing praise or compliments; complimentary
The actor's apartment was filled with laudatory reviews he had clipped from various newspapers over the years.

lavish (LA-vish), adjective or verb
Abundant and overflowing; extravagant; excessively lush (adjective) or to shower with abundance; to give without reserve (verb)
The gardens at Versailles in France are known throughout the world as being some of the most lavish and beautiful ever grown.
As an aunt, the woman considered it her responsibility to lavish her nephews with not only love but adventure as well.

legacy (LEG-ah-see), noun
Anything, material or otherwise, handed down from one generation to the next
The United States has a long legacy of protecting the rights and freedoms of individuals.

lenient (LEE-nee-uhnt) or (LEEN-yunht), adjective
Permissive and indulgent; inclined not to be harsh or strict
While some children need structure and strict discipline, others thrive under more lenient situations where they can make their own decisions.

lethargic (leh-THAR-jik), adjective
Lacking in energy; tired; slow and sluggish
She knew her son was sick when he was achy and lethargic and didn't mind staying in bed on a Saturday.

levee (LEH-vee), noun
A structure built to hold back a body of water; a dike; a barrier created to prevent an area from being flooded by a river or sea

When the levees collapsed in 2005, the city of New Orleans was devastated by the rising sea waters.

levity (LEHV-ih-tee), noun
Humor or a joking manner, often in an inappropriate place or time; amusement; foolishness

His attempt to inject some levity into the emergency meeting was met with disapproval and a concern that he wasn't taking the matter seriously.

lexicon (LEKS-ih-kon), noun
The vocabulary or words used by a specific group or within a specific field

One of the many difficulties faced by adults is keeping up with the current and ever-changing lexicon of teenagers.

libel (LIY-buhl), noun or verb
Any publication, be it written word or picture, that is false and damaging to a person's reputation or well-being (noun) or to write or publish lies or other false information about a person (verb)

Tabloid magazines must be careful when printing rumors because they can be sued for libel if the information is not true.

The bloggers didn't care if they were libeling the candidate or not so long as what they wrote contributed to her losing the election.

licentious (LIY-sen-shus), adjective
Having little or no care for rules and morals when it comes to sexual behaviors

In this day and age of AIDS and other STDs, licentious behavior can result in more than just a bad reputation.

lien (LEEN), noun
The legal right to hold a person's property until a debt is paid

The bank had a lien on the couple's house in case they could not pay back the loan.

linger (LIHN-ger), verb
To stay in a place longer than necessary, usually because of a reluctance to leave; to take one's time; or to hang around; to persist

He lingered outside his classroom hoping to catch a glimpse of the teacher he had a crush on.

The young man smiled when he realized his girlfriend's perfume was still lingering in his car even after he had taken her home.

listless (LIST-luhs), adjective
Having no energy or enthusiasm; uncaring and disinterested; having low spirits

She was listless for weeks after the breakup until her friends finally took her out for a night on the town so she could enjoy life again.

lithe (LIYTH), adjective
Graceful, moving with ease; flexible; limber; willowy

Her lithe movements and constant poise marked her as a dancer even when she was offstage.

lobbyist (LAH-bee-ist), noun
A professional hired by a group to persuade politicians to pass laws and regulations the group favors

His concern for the environment, along with his ability to be persuasive, made him an excellent lobbyist for conservation groups.

lofty (LAWF-tee), adjective
Very tall or very high; imposing; or noble; of high character; impressive and respectable; or self-important; arrogant; pompous

The lofty buildings towered over the small church in the center of the square.

His lofty ideas could never have been realized without his partner's common sense and business skills.

In fairy tales, evil stepmothers often treat the heroine with lofty distain if not downright cruelty.

longevity (lon-JEHV-ih-tee), noun
Long life; duration, usually of life; or an overly long period of time within a position or situation

Doctors are striving not just to achieve longevity but also a good quality of life for their patients.

Her longevity with the company was rewarded with a huge retirement party and a substantial pension.

loquacious (loh-KWAY-shus), adjective
Talkative; excessively wordy; prone to going on and on

The professor was so loquacious it was difficult for students to separate the important facts from fluff.

lucid (LOO-sid), adjective
Clear and easy to understand; well explained or thought out; or sane and mentally stable, used to describe moments between bouts of delusion or unconsciousness; aware of one's surroundings and situation

The defendant's explanation of his alibi was lucid but strangely emotionless and dry considering what was at stake.

Even though she was perfectly lucid, the EMTs took her to the hospital for observation after she hit her head.

luminary (LOO-mih-nayr-ee), noun
A person who inspires or influences others, often but not necessarily in a specific group; or a celestial object that gives off natural light

Many political leaders from the twentieth century will be luminaries to the leaders of future generations.

The earth's sun is the most well-known and recognizable luminary in the galaxy.

lurid (LYOO-rid), adjective
Shocking, explicit, or gruesome; graphic beyond necessity; or glaringly ornate; overdone with color, usually creating an unnatural, often unpleasant effect

Although the mainstream media showed tact in reporting the crime, the tabloids published all the lurid details.

The colors chosen for the playground turned out to be lurid and slightly eerie instead of bright and happy as intended.

M

lustrous (LUHS-trus), adjective
Glowing, as from an inner light; shining and bright; having a soft light
The snow and the full moon gave the gardens a lustrous, romantic look that made them perfect for the couple's date, in spite of the cold.

luxuriant (lug-ZHOOR-ee-ant), adjective
Thick and healthy growth; lush; or characterized by luxury; decadent and delightful
The young man's thick, luxuriant hair made him the envy of most women who knew him.
The woman couldn't believe she actually owned something as luxuriant as her new cashmere robe.

malcontent (MAL-kon-tent), noun or adjective
A person who is discontented or unhappy, generally with the government and the status quo and makes those views known thorough words and actions; a rebel (noun) or dissatisfied and disgusted, especially with authority or the government; discontented (adjective)
The protestors spoke calmly and rationally in order to be taken seriously and to avoid being seen as a group of malcontents.
Many analysts predicted malcontent Democrats would vote for a third-party candidate in order to make a statement about the new party platform.

Similar but Not the Same
Two words with similar meanings are not always interchangeable. This is the case for malevolent (muh-LEHV-oh-lent) and malicious (muh-LISH-us). The word malevolent describes someone who is generally cruel or nasty. A malevolent person doesn't care or hold a grudge against any particular person. On the other hand, malicious describes someone who is mean or hurtful to a specific person or about a specific thing.

---

malevolent (muh-LEHV-oh-lent), adjective
Characterized by having, showing, or carrying ill-will and a desire to do harm to others; evil; wishing others harm
All of the great villains in fiction have a malevolent streak in them that becomes focused most strongly on the hero.

malicious (muh-LISH-us), adjective
Deliberately and intentionally harmful; knowingly hurtful and damaging
   Although she claimed her statements had not been malicious, but simply misunderstood, no one who knew her true feelings believed her.

malign (MUH-liyn), verb or adjective
To make intentionally harmful, cruel, and often untrue statements about a person; to criticize in an intentionally harsh or hurtful way (verb) or influential in an evil way; characterized by having evil nature or intent (adjective)
   The star was grateful for her friends who stood by her when the press maligned her for unpopular statements she had allegedly made in college.
   The witches in the play Macbeth are considered to have a malign influence over the lead characters.

malleable (MAH-lee-ah-bul), adjective
Able to shape and form without breaking, referring to a substance; or unformed; impressionable; easily swayed or taught; able to be manipulated
   Even the hardest steel becomes malleable when heated above a certain temperature.
   The professor enjoyed teaching philosophy to freshman because their ideas were fresh and their minds still malleable.

manifest (MAN-ih-fehst), adjective, verb, or noun
Plainly and clearly obvious; easily seen or understood (adjective) or to express, show, or reveal; to personify by one's actions; to demonstrate (verb) or the list of cargo and/or passengers on a ship or plane (noun)
   The glaring error in the headline was so manifest to everyone, the editor knew someone would be fired for missing it before the paper went to print.
   Although emotions may manifest differently in different people, even the most subdued or private person has feelings.
   The captain checked off the manifest several times to ensure everything was on board before sailing on the long ocean voyage.

manumit (man-yoo-MIHT), verb
To set free, as from slavery, bondage, or servitude
   Most human rights watch groups believe that no human is truly free until all slaves are manumit and free to live as human beings and not property.

M

mar (MAHR), verb or noun
To damage or disfigure; to spoil or cause harm to something (verb) or a mark or spot that spoils the overall look, situation, or experience (noun)

The bride refused to let a few clouds and light sprinkles mar the overall beauty of her wedding day.

Due to a mar on the back of the cabinet, she was able to buy it at well under normal retail price.

martial (MAR-shul), adjective
Having to do with or regarding war or soldiering; suggestive of war and/or being a soldier; warlike; soldier-like

The search and rescue team showed martial courage, risking their own lives to save people trapped by the storm.

maudlin (MAWD-lin), adjective
Excessively sentimental, usually to the point of tears, often involving an element of self-pity; weepy for sad, sentimental, and perhaps self-absorbed reasons; often associated with drunkenness

No one enjoyed her company after her third drink because she became maudlin talking about her years as a young dancer and what could have been.

maverick (MA-ver-ik), noun or adjective
A freethinking, slightly rebellious person; a person who refuses to conform to a particular idea or standard; or a calf or other livestock that has yet to be branded, traditionally considered the property of whoever first brands it if it roams free (noun) or independent and freethinking; slightly radical or rebellious (adjective)

People who truly want to make their mark on the world and society cannot be afraid to be labeled mavericks by those who are happy with the way things have always been.

The rancher always kept a close eye on his mavericks so no other rancher could brand them and claim them.

His maverick attitude toward the criminal justice system made him a popular, if unpredictable, judge.

M

mawkish (MAW-kish), adjective
Sentimental in a sappy, even offensive way; sickly sweet emotion
It was difficult to buy his grandmother a Mother's Day card because most of them were so mawkish that they didn't fit her straightforward personality.

meander (mee-AN-dehr), verb
To move or flow in a random path; to wander aimlessly without a set direction
The young couple chose to meander through the gardens, holding hands and enjoying each other's company, rather than head straight back to the dorms.

mellifluous (muh-LIF-loo-uhs), adjective
Pleasant sounding; flowing and musical sounding; flowing sweetly, smoothly
The overnight DJ's mellifluous voice helped soothe many people who were restless and could not sleep during the long, dark nights.

mendacity (men-DAS-ih-tee), noun
Lies; untruthfulness; dishonesty
She was often amazed at the mendacity that would come from her brother's mouth and more so that her parents would believe him.

mendicant (MEN-dih-kuhnt), adjective or noun
Dependent upon alms or charity for a living (adjective) or one who asks for alms or charity, usually a man from a religious group, in order to live (noun)
In the Middle Ages, the mendicant religious orders could face hard, poor winters if people had not shown them charity during the previous seasons.
The mendicant traveled from town to town, stopping to preach wherever he would be given some food and a little money.

mercenary (MUR-seh-nar-ee), adjective or noun
Solely interested in monetary gain, even at the expense of morals and ethics (adjective) or a soldier hired by another country who is interested only in the money offered, not the politics or ideals involved (noun)
He bought and sold companies with a mercenary indifference to the employees or their families.
Generally speaking, mercenaries do not fight with the same heart as the soldiers who are fighting for their homes and their country.

M

meretricious (mayr-eh-TRISH-us), adjective
Attractive on the surface but having no real value; attracting attention in a gaudy and flashy way; or reasonable to believe yet insincere and fake; phony, referring to an argument

Every summer, the beaches are filled with stalls selling meretricious souvenirs to the tourists.

She never quite believed his meretricious statements of friendship even though others called her cynical.

mesmerize (MEZ-mer-iyz), adjective
To entrance or enthrall; to hypnotize; to strongly attract

The young girls were mesmerized by the colors, lights, and sounds of their first performance of the ballet.

meticulous (meh-TIK-yoo-lus), adjective
Having or showing great concern for details; taking great care; being precise

The young woman's meticulous nature was evident by how clean her room and desk were even in the middle of finals.

mettle (MEH-tul), noun
The ability to cope well with adversity or challenges; courage; spirit and heart; the ability to rise to an occasion

The runner showed his true mettle when he managed to qualify for the competition even though he tripped during trials.

mettlesome (MEH-tul-som), adjective
Having an unbroken spirit; characterized by courage and heart

The mettlesome soccer team managed to play their way into the finals in spite of injuries and other setbacks.

microcosm (MIYK-roh-kah-zim), noun
A situation, community, or system that represents a larger whole; a smaller, representative sample

College campuses, with their diverse populations, politics, and hierarchies, are microcosms of society at large.

M

mien (MEEN), adjective
Bearing or conduct; look or appearance, especially as it relates to personality or character
The dean's austere mien caused most students to avoid dealing with him directly.

mirth (MERTH), noun
Great joy, happiness, and cheer, especially expressed through laughter
For many people, the Christmas holidays are a time of mirth, friendship, and giving thanks for one another.

misanthrope (MIS-ahn-throhp), noun
Someone who dislikes humanity and people in general
She claimed to be a misanthrope but her friends knew she had just been hurt badly by an old boyfriend.

mischievous (MIS-chihv-us), adjective
Playful in a naughty manner; having a fondness for causing trouble in a cheerful and prankish way
His mischievous sense of humor and the twinkle in his eye got him into—and out of—trouble as a teenager.

miscreant (MIS-kree-ant), noun
Someone who behaves badly; a person who breaks the law or behaves in other socially unacceptable ways
Although he was trying to be tough and cool, he only succeeded in getting himself a reputation as a miscreant.

miser (MIY-zur), noun
A person, usually wealthy, who saves money to an extreme degree; someone who spends as little money as possible for the purpose of keeping the wealth
Ebenezer Scrooge was well-known as a miser until the ghosts taught him there was more to life than money.

miserly (MIY-zur-lee), adjective
Characterized by greediness, lack of generosity, or penny-pinching
The miserly old landlady kept them all cold in the winter because she didn't want to pay a high heating bill.

misnomer (mis-NOH-mer), noun
An unsuitable and incorrect or misleading name for any given object
Considering the length of the wait at many drive-thrus, "fast food" is quickly becoming a misnomer.

mitigate (MIT-ih-gayt), verb
To make easier; to soothe; to alleviate; to lessen a burden
The pain of losing first place was mitigated when she overheard her father praising her performance anyway.

moderation (mod-eh-RAY-shun), noun
Characterized by not being at either extreme; an avoidance of excess
It was difficult for her to eat ice cream in moderation, especially in the summer with a shop open on almost every corner.

modicum (MOH-dih-kum), noun
A small amount, often used when describing something valuable or desired; a token or trivial amount
As sad as her stories sometimes were, there was always at least a modicum of humor in each that could make people smile.

mollify (MAWL-ih-fiy), noun
To soften temper or anger; to soothe anxiety; to relieve tension in a situation
Whenever the clerks needed to mollify a customer, they always called on Tom because he was the most diplomatic of all of the employees.

molt (MOHLT), verb
To shed skin, fur, feathers, or other outer covering in order to allow new growth
The Saint Bernard shed often, but in the spring when it was time for him to molt, the house was positively covered in fur.

monolithic (mon-oh-LITH-ik), adjective
Massive and imposing in size, either literal or figurative, when literal, often formed from a single piece of stone or other material; large, solid, and imposing
The monolithic doors leading into the capitol building left many visitors stunned and in awe.

M

monomania (mon-uh-MAY-nee-ya), noun
An obsession or intense preoccupation with a single subject matter
  Her parents were concerned that her interest in religion was beginning to shift into monomania.

mordant (MOHR-dnt), adjective
Sharp, sarcastic, and piercing, used when describing wit or humor
  The comedian's mordant observations made people recognize the truth in his statements even as they made people laugh.

morose (muh-ROHS), adjective
Dejected or downhearted in a sullen, moody way; moody and depressed; brooding
  He became so morose when he wasn't accepted to his first choice of college that no one wanted to approach him for weeks.

mosaic (moh-ZAY-ik), noun
A piece of artwork created by attaching pieces of glass, tile, stone, or other substance on a surface in a pattern or design
  The mosaic that hung over her bed was made from sea glass she had collected while vacationing in the Caribbean.

multifarious (muhl-tuh-FAYR-ree-uhs), adjective
Extremely diverse; having many aspects to its nature; created from differing parts
  Immigrants to the United States are, to this day, often drawn to New York City because of its multifarious and multicultural nature.

munificent (myoo-NIHF-ih-sint), adjective
Showing great and overwhelming generosity; giving liberally
  The critics were munificent in their praise for the child actor who had taken on such a challenging role.

myriad (meer-REE-ad), adjective
An enormous amount; an incalculable amount; an indefinite number
  The stores at the mall had a myriad of choices for the young women shopping for prom dresses.

nadir (NAY-der), noun
In astronomy, the point directly underneath the observer on the sphere; or the lowest point possible; extreme adversity; the rock bottom
From the North Pole, the South Pole is the nadir of planet earth.
Running out of gas and having to walk three miles in her dress shoes had to be the nadir of a very bad night.

nascent (NAY-suhnt), adjective
Just coming to be; newly but not yet fully developed; beginning to grow and show signs of potential; generally used when describing a process or organization
Many common items people take for granted today, such as the computer and cell phones, were only nascent technologies as recently as the 1980s.

nebulous (NEB-yoo-lus), adjective
Foggy, cloudy, or hazy; unclear and undefined; blurred; indistinct; may be used literally to describe atmosphere or figuratively to describe concepts, words, or ideas
His brothers refused to sneak out with him because the plan for getting past their parents' bedroom was nebulous at best.

nefarious (neh-FAYR-ree-us), adjective
Wicked or evil; villainous; may imply infamous as well as cruel
The documentary focused on the nefarious crimes of serial killers in the twentieth century.

neologism (nee-AWL-eh-jizm), noun
A word or phrase that has just been created; "to coin a phrase"; a new word
The advancements, slang, and discoveries of every generation have added neologisms that become commonplace in the language used by ordinary people.

noisome (NOY-suhm), adjective
Offensive and foul; harmful, possibly toxic; usually used when describing an odor, smell, or fumes
The lab was filled with a noisome odor for days after the student spilled the formaldehyde during an experiment.

nominal (NAH-mih-nuhl), adjective

Insignificant, trifling, or token; or existing for show but having no real depth; or lower than actual or expected value; or having to do with a specific name

The attorney charged her friend only a nominal fee because she knew drawing up the will would take very little time.

His girlfriend only showed a nominal interest in football so he finally stopped trying to explain the rules to her.

The service at the restaurant was so poor that the couple only left a nominal tip for the server.

He would only donate to the building fund if the college promised to give the building an anonymous title rather than a nominal one identifying him as the donor.

nostrum (NOH-strum), noun

Any medicine with unknown ingredients and results; usually fake medicine that promises the quick fix; medicine touted by its creator as a cure-all but with no scientific backing or proof; or a popular but unproven or ineffective solution to problems or evils

Even though the pill was a nostrum, its makers guaranteed it would cause weight loss so people spent huge amounts of money on it.

Boot camps for troubled teens are a nostrum for juvenile delinquency but their long-term effectiveness is still unknown.

notoriety (no-ter-RIY-ih-tee), noun

Being known for an undesirable reason

She could have lived without the notoriety that resulted from being asked to testify in front of the honor board.

nugatory (NOO-guh-tor-ee), adjective

Insignificant; having little importance; pointless or without purpose; or ineffective or meaningless; powerless; figuratively, without teeth; worthless

The world ignored Hitler's earliest writings as nugatory but quickly realized this had been a mistake of enormous proportions.

Some people are beginning to wonder if the speed limit has become a nugatory law considering most people drive very fast on highways and interstates regardless.

obdurate (AHB-dur-iht), adjective
Stubborn and refusing to change, especially when faced with a gentler or more compassionate option

King Henry VIII was obdurate in his decision that his enemies be executed, refusing even to meet with them or read their letters after their imprisonment.

obfuscate (AHB-fyoo-skayt), verb
To intentionally make something unclear or confusing; to purposefully make facts or a situation difficult to understand

The principal wasn't sure if the young man was just confused about the facts or if he was trying to obfuscate the story in order to protect his friends.

obstreperous (uhb-STREP-er-us), adjective
Stubborn to the point of defiance; intentionally difficult to handle; noisy and aggressive

The teenagers were obstreperous when they were together but once their teacher separated them, each one settled down.

obtrude (ub-TROOD), verb
To intrude or become noticeable in an unpleasant, unwelcome way; to force upon

The roommates' lifestyles threatened to obtrude upon each other until the young women came up with an arrangement that respected everyone's rights and feelings.

obviate (AHB-vee-ayt), verb
To get rid of, eliminate, or make unnecessary; to do away with a need or necessity; or to prevent from occurring; to forestall

He soon discovered working at the daycare obviated his need for extra time in the gym.

Seatbelts can obviate serious injury in the case of a car accident.

occlude (uh-KLOOD), verb
To obscure or block the path of; or to stop up, close, or make unpassable

She bought the tickets to see her favorite band even though the sight line was occluded.

Once the doctors realized the patient's arteries were occluded, a proper course of treatment could begin.

odious (OH-dee-us), adjective
Disgusting, repellant, reprehensible; causing extreme dislike or displeasure
She was shocked that in spite of the odious way her brother treated women, he always seemed to have a girlfriend.

odium (OH-dee-yum), noun
Contempt and disgust for a person, concept, or idea, often widespread and commonly felt
The odium felt for telemarketers makes it that much more difficult for them to perform their jobs well.

officious (oh-FISH-us), adjective
Overly eager to offer advice or assistance, to the point of being annoying; intrusively helpful, especially regarding trivial matters
She cringed when she realized the person assigned to her department was the man everyone considered an officious know-it-all.

ominous (AH-mih-nus), adjective
Hinting at something evil or dangerous; presenting a feeling of foreboding; eerie
The tree-lined shortcut was perfectly safe during the day but always felt ominous after dark.

onus (OH-nus), noun
A difficult responsibility or duty; obligation; burden of proof
The onus was on the teacher to prove the two students had cheated on their exams.

opportunist (opp-er-TOON-ist), noun
A person who takes advantage of a situation to achieve his or her own goals, regardless of the consequences
She was accused of being an opportunist when she applied for the position before the vacancy was even made public.

opprobrium (uh-PROH-bree-um), noun

Harsh and scornful criticism; extreme disapproval; or disgrace and shame created by acting in a particularly dishonorable way, usually a public disgrace

Her bigoted and close-minded statements were met with opprobrium from every organization in the school.

The scandal caused him such opprobrium that the senator chose to resign from Congress and retire from public life.

orator (OR-ay-tor), noun

A skilled public speaker; one who makes speeches

The candidate was an eloquent and charismatic orator who could impress even his staunchest critics.

ornate (or-NAYT), adjective

Highly decorated; showy, flashy and intricate; heavily ornamented; or flowery and complex, referring to writing style

The ornate picture frame displayed in the window looked out of place in the run-down junk shop.

Freshmen often try to impress their professors with an ornate writing style but the smart students learn that this usually has the opposite effect.

oscillate (AHS-uh-layt), verb

To swing steadily at an uninterrupted pace; to move back and forth at a regular speed; or to be unable to decide between two choices; to waver between separate and often opposing ideas

She bought a fan that oscillated in order to cool more of the overheated room.

Politicians are known to sometimes oscillate on hot-button issues, depending on the politics of the group they are addressing at the time.

ossify (AWH-sih-fiy), verb

To become set in one's ways; to become rigid and unwilling or unable to change; to become unalterable

The man's attitudes had begun to ossify in his fifties so by the time he was old, he wouldn't even listen to other ideas or arguments.

ostracism (AWHS-trah-sih-zum), noun
The act of banishing a person or subgroup from a larger group or community
Although she had been right to report the cheating, the ostracism she faced afterward made it very difficult to believe she had acted wisely.

ostracize (AWHS-trah-sihz), verb
To banish or exclude, from a group, community, or society
Sadly, many countries around the world still ostracize people with physical, mental, and emotional disabilities.

pacifist (PAS-ih-fist), noun
A person who believes that war and violence cannot ever be justified under any circumstance and that all disagreements can and should be settled in a nonviolent way
As a pacifist, she often got into debates regarding the necessity of even having a military, let alone going to war.

paean (PEE-uhn), noun
A song or other expression of great joy and praise
His writings were practically a paean to fatherhood and the pleasure he took in raising his children.

Watch Out!

Adding a suffix is a simple way to change the part of speech of many words. It seems obvious that pollute and pollution are related words. But it's not always that simple. Although palate and palatial appear to be different forms of the same word, they really are not. Palate (PAHL-eht) is the roof of the mouth or an appreciation for something. Palatial (puh-LAY-shul) means easily compared to a palace.

---

palate (PAHL-eht), noun
The roof of the mouth; or appreciation for; taste or liking
She burned her palate as well as her tongue gulping the hot coffee too quickly.
He developed a refined palate after months of eating in the finest restaurants in Paris.

palatial (puh-LAY-shul), adjective
Easily compared to a palace; large and impressive
The realtor knew that the palatial estate would sell quickly.

palliate (PAHL-ee-ayt), verb
To make a crime or wrongdoing less severe, serious, or harsh; or to moderate or alleviate, generally fears, concerns, or suspicions; or to remove the symptoms of a disease or an illness without providing a cure
The attorney argued that the defendant's history of abuse and neglect should serve to palliate the crime.
The babysitter tried to palliate the young couple's concerns about going out without the baby for the first time.
Cold medicines effectively palliate most characteristics of the cold so a person can continue to function even while sick.

palpable (PAL-puh-bul), adjective
Able to be felt, touched, or seen by humans; tangible; or so intense, it can practically be felt, touched, or seen; or obvious, plain, clearly seen
When the baby first kicked, the young parents were thrilled to have palpable evidence of its health and well-being.
The love between her grandparents was palpable to anyone who spent more than five minutes in their presence.
Although the scratches were palpable, he couldn't get his head around the fact that someone had vandalized his brand-new car.

panacea (pan-ah-SEE-ah), noun
A cure or remedy for every ailment or discomfort
In his grandmother's opinion, a strong cup of tea was the panacea, regardless of the problem.

panegyric (pan-ih-JIHR-ik) or (pan-ih-JIY-rik), noun or adjective
A formal statement of praise, usually made in the form of a public speech or a published work (noun) or praising; highly complimentary (adjective)
The actor took out a full page ad as a panegyric about how he had enjoyed working with his costar on their latest movie.
The panegyric nature of the dean's introduction of her son made the woman swell with pride and happiness.

panoply (PAN-ah-plee), noun

A large, sometimes complete, impressive display or collection; or complete ceremonial attire; or a protective covering

The opening ceremony of the Olympics creates the magnificent panoply of colors and sounds as the nations of the world gather to celebrate and compete.

The prince rarely appeared in full panoply, preferring instead to wear a plain black, pinstripe suit to most functions.

The spiky panoply of a cactus makes an inconvenient source of food or water for desert animals.

pariah (puh-RIY-ah), noun

A social outcast; one who is completely rejected from a community or a society at large

Many whistleblowers discover they have suddenly become pariahs in the same cities and towns where they were once well-respected members of the community.

paroxysm (PAHR-oks-izm), noun

A sudden and unexpected display of emotion; or an unexpected convulsion, generally related to a disease or illness

His story was so funny that his friends were all in the grip of paroxysms of laughter by the end of it.

The paroxysm was brought on when the doctors could not lower the child's fever.

partisan (PAHR-tih-zen), noun or adjective

An avid and devout follower of a group, cause, or political party (noun) or devoted to a particular cause to the point of being biased against anything else (adjective)

The partisans following the general were willing to risk their lives to bring him to power.

His partisan devotion to human rights and heartfelt speeches made him a leader many oppressed people could believe in and follow.

pathos (PAY-thohs) or (PAY-thuhs), noun
A certain quality or experience that invokes or creates feelings of pity and sympathy, often used to describe a reaction to artwork; or the pity and sympathy created by such art

No one in the audience was immune to the pathos of the ballet's death scene as the beautiful swan danced her last dance and died.

His pathos at the sight of the painting soon turned to amusement when he discovered it hadn't been drawn by one of the masters but by a seven-year-old girl.

peccadillo (pek-uh-DIL-oh), noun
A small, virtually insignificant error; a petty misdeed or sin

An action that for a common man would be considered a peccadillo can become a scandal when performed by a world leader.

pedagogy (ped-ih-GAH-gee) or (ped-ih-GOH-gee), noun
The method and principles of teaching, especially subjects requiring intellectual thought as opposed to straight facts or rote learning; or the teaching profession, especially at postsecondary levels

She grasped philosophy so quickly that her professors were shocked that these were her first experiences with philosophical pedagogy.

Although he had never expected to go into pedagogy, teaching at the seminary was a logical progression in his career.

pedantic (ped-DAN-tik), adjective
Characterized by a narrow, somewhat petty, attention to facts and book learning; focused only on the trivial facts of a certain topic; marked by a tiresome need to prove book smarts about a topic

The lecturer's pedantic style bored those in the field and simply confused those who weren't in the field.

pellucid (peh-LOO-sid), adjective
Clear, see-through, admitting light; able to look through; or easy to understand; clearly stated; plain and obvious

The pellucid waters surrounding the island revealed a host of sea life not common in lakes or rivers.

The author's pellucid style won her critical praise but the public found her work to be sparse and cold.

penchant (PEN-chuhnt), noun
A strong liking; an intense but healthy interest in a subject matter; a tendency to participate in a specific event with gusto and enjoyment

In spite of his academic, slightly nerdy appearance, he had a strong penchant for sports, following his favorite teams closely every season.

penurious (PEH-nyoo-ree-us) or (PEH-noo-ree-us), adjective
Very poor, bordering on destitute; unable to pay for common necessities; or unwilling to spend money for indulgences; stingy; or barren or unfertile; not productive; can be used literally to describe land or figuratively to describe a mindset

In spite of America's overall wealth, there are still many penurious communities where whole neighborhoods and towns struggle simply to survive.

Her penurious ways had made her very wealthy but she had little to show for it besides a large bank account.

His penurious thought process was not up to the challenge of coming up with creative ways to solve the company's financial woes.

penury (PEN-yeh-ree), noun
Destitution; extreme poverty; financial want; or barrenness; having no resources or ability; infertile

Few tourists to resort islands ever see the penury in which most locals live their day-to-day lives.

In spite of the farmer's best efforts, the penury of the fields would simply not produce the crops he had hoped for.

peregrination (pehr-uh-gruh-NAY-shun), noun
A trip taken by foot; a traveling or wandering, usually by foot

Instead of a whirlwind tour of Europe, the friends decided on a slower but more in-depth peregrination of the French countryside.

peremptory (peh-REMP-toh-ree), adjective
Refusing to allow debate, conversation, or refusal; requiring immediate attention and action without question; or urgent; characterized by being a command,
not a request; or offensively arrogant and self-assured; bossy; self-important

*Even more than his rank, the drill sergeant's peremptory tone and attitude
made the new recruits fall in line.*

*Their boss was so laid-back that on the rare occasions she used a peremptory
tone, no one even considered arguing with her.*

*His peremptory attitude had put off so many people that none of his coworkers
felt sorry for him when he was publicly chastised for losing the account.*

perennial (per-EHN-ee-uhl), adjective or noun
Lasting for a long period of time, perhaps even indefinitely; rejuvenating or
reoccurring (adjective) or a plant that grows three or more seasons; or anything that reoccurs year after year (noun)

*Eating properly and exercising are two known keys to perennial health and
longevity.*

*She didn't have much time to garden so she planted perennials, knowing they
would bloom year after year.*

*The Thanksgiving Day Parade is a trusted perennial and, for many families,
signifies the start of the holiday season.*

perfidy (PUR-fih-dee), noun
Treason or treachery; a deliberate and intentional breach of trust; an act of
betrayal

*As Benedict Arnold learned, one act of perfidy is enough to erase years of loy-
alty and devotion to a cause.*

perfunctory (per-FUNK-tuh-ree), adjective
Managed or handled without care or particular thought; done because it has
to be done, not because it is cared about; phoned in; done with indifference

*The bored clerk gave a perfunctory glance at the paperwork before automati-
cally forwarding it on to the next department.*

peripatetic (pehr-ih-peh-TET-ik), adjective
Moving about; changing locations frequently; staying in place for short periods of time; traveling, traditionally by foot but common usage is more generalized
Growing up in a military family, his childhood was peripatetic so he was often the new kid on the block.

peripheral (peh-RIF-er-uhl), adjective
On the edge; regarding the outer limits or boundaries; or being a secondary or less important concern; of less importance; not the main focus
The peripheral suburbs of the city were popular because rents were much lower but downtown was still easily accessible.
Many parents encourage their children to focus on grades and attendance instead of worrying about peripheral concerns while they are still in school.

permeate (PER-mee-ayt), verb
To fill a space; to spread throughout; to flow or pass through
The excitement leading up to graduation had permeated the whole school, so that even the teachers seemed happier and more enthusiastic.

pernicious (pur-NIH-shus), adjective
Harmful in a slow, subtle way; dangerous and sly at the same time; causing damage in a slow, constant way; or deadly; highly destructive
The pernicious rumors about her, though false, managed to undermine her chances for promotion.
The doctors prescribed an aggressive course of treatment to counteract the pernicious disease.

perpetuate (per-PEHT-yoo-ayt), verb
To prolong or cause to continue; to keep something going, usually an attitude or belief
Glamour and fashion magazines risk perpetuating an ideal of feminine beauty that very few real women can ever hope to achieve.

persiflage (PUR-suh-flahgz), noun
Pleasant, joking chatter; gentle and good-natured teasing; lighthearted mockery; or a lighthearted, easy way of discussing even serious matters

The man was so well-respected that the jokes and stories told at his retirement ceremony never crossed beyond persiflage.

The same persiflage that made the reporter so good with human interest stories prevented him from ever making anchor and tackling hard-hitting news stories.

perturbation (pur-tur-BAY-shun), noun
Anxiety; the state of being worried or disturbed; uneasiness

The young dancer often wondered if the perturbation caused by auditions was worth the chance to land a Broadway role.

peruse (peh-ROOZ), verb
To read, examine, or study with great care and attention to detail; to study thoroughly

She knew she couldn't just skim the text but would need to peruse it if she was going to pass the test.

pervade (per-VAYD), verb
To exist throughout; to spread completely

A sense of panic began to pervade the freshman dorms as the students got closer and closer to their first set of finals.

pessimism (PES-ih-mih-zim), noun
A gloomy mindset; the habit of seeing only the negative aspects of things; an attitude that the worst will always come of every situation

Although her friends tried to be understanding, her constant pessimism made her difficult and depressing to be around for very long.

petrified (PEHT-trih-fiyd), adjective
Frightened or scared to the point of being unable to move, function, or think; or to turn an organic matter, such as wood, into a stonelike substance, generally caused by great lengths of time and pressure

Ever since she had been a child, the very thought of, let alone the presence of, spiders had petrified her.

The stone in her mother's necklace was actually petrified wood, polished to a high shine.

petulant
Petty, childish, and sullen; demandingly pouty
The spoiled little boy grew up to be a petulant man who couldn't take no for an answer and always expected to get his way.

phenomena (fih-NOM-ih-nah), noun
Unusual, extraordinary events or happenings; significant and remarkable occurrences; the plural of phenomenon; or any happenings, occurrences, or events that can be recognized by any of the five senses
The strange lights and colors that appeared over the town during the week were phenomena that no scientist could every truly explain.
After his ear surgery, he was struck by the phenomena of sounds as he heard them for the first time in his life.

Goose, Geese, Moose . . . Meese?

Some plurals aren't as simple as adding an s or es to the end of a word. A phenomenon (fih-NOM-ih-non) is one extraordinary event. But two or more extraordinary events are phenomena (fih-NOM-ih-nah). Therefore, a single UFO is a phenomenon. Three sightings of UFOs are phenomena. The first means there is only one, while the second indicates more than one.

philanthropist (fih-LAN-throh-pist), noun
A person who donates money, time, and resources to improve the overall welfare of humanity
He became a philanthropist after making his first million as a way to give back to the world that had given him so much.

phlegmatic (fleg-MA-tik), adjective
Having an even, level temperament; unemotional; calm and difficult to fluster
Her phlegmatic nature made her an excellent police officer because she kept her head no matter what the crisis.

physiognomy (fiz-ee-OG-noh-mee), noun
The facial features, generally used when using the facial features to tell a person's character or ethnic background; or the skill of reading or judging a person by his or her facial features; or the overall features, character, and look of any particular subject, living or nonliving
Subtle differences exist in the physiognomy of the various races and ethnicities found throughout the world.
Skilled in physiognomy after years of listening to students' excuses and rationales, most teachers can tell when someone is lying.
The physiognomy of the American Southwest is usually exactly what tourists hope it will be: warm, wide open, and full of friendly, welcoming people.

piety (PIY-eh-tee), noun
The state of being religious, faithful, and devout
The priest's piety was balanced by his sense of humor and willingness to listen.

pious (PIY-us), adjective
Having extreme religious devotion and faith; marked by a strict moral code, usually based on religious belief; or marked by false faith or hypocritical devotion; falsely devout; or commendable, admirable, and honorable; praiseworthy
The woman's pious nature led her to consider becoming a nun.
His pious anger toward the hate crime managed to insult the people who truly followed the faith.
The man's pious efforts to quit drinking finally paid off when he celebrated his one-year anniversary of not drinking alcohol.

pique (PEEK), verb or noun
To make someone feel irritated or put out; to wound someone's pride; or to create, stir up, or arouse; or to pride oneself on (verb) or a feeling of irritation or being put out, caused by a perceived slight or insult (noun)
She unintentionally piqued her neighbors when she didn't invite them to her annual Halloween party.
The staff's interest was piqued by the arrival of a dozen red roses for the young woman who worked in the mailroom.
He piqued himself on his ability to get along with anyone and fit into any crowd.
Her pique at not being elected homecoming queen quickly dissolved when the young man she was interested in asked her to dance.

pitfall (PIT-fal), noun

An unrecognized or hidden source of trouble, difficulty, or danger; or a covered hole in the ground acting as a trap

It was his job to be on the lookout for any pitfall that could delay the completion of the project.

The tiger ran straight into the pitfall the hunters had dug when they realized it was on the hunt in the area.

pith (PIHTH), noun

The white, spongy lining inside the rind of many citrus fruits; or the soft center of the stem of a plant; or the heart of the matter; the essence or core of a thought, concept, or idea; the important part

Although the flesh of an orange is sweet, many people find the pith to be a bitter distraction.

The cat had chewed the plants down to their pith before anyone noticed it was happening.

The pith of the speech was hidden among flowery language and fawning compliments.

platitude (PLA-tih-tood), noun

A statement that has been used so often it has lost any meaning or significance; a cliché; an unoriginal, obvious remark or observation, often made as if it were original or meaningful

The grieving widow had to fight to keep her patience when insensitive people offered her platitudes instead of sincerity.

plenary (PLEH-neh-ree), adjective or noun

Entire and complete; full; without reservation; or attended by all members and qualified participants (adjective) or a meeting attended by all members, who would otherwise meet in smaller committees on a more regular basis (noun)

The United States government is a three-branch system with checks and balances built in so not even the president has plenary powers.

It was difficult to find a time to hold the plenary meeting because so many people's schedules had to be considered.

She enjoyed attending the plenary because it gave her a chance to see other people involved in the organization who were not on her committee.

plethora (PLETH-uh-rah), noun
Excess; overabundance; an embarrassing amount

The house manager rolled his eyes at the plethora of demands made by the diva performing later in the week.

plumb (PLUM), verb, noun, adjective, or adverb
To figure out the depth or vertical alignment using a specific piece of metal; or to make straight; or to explore or experience completely; or to be employed or perform the work of a plumber (verb) or a metal weight at the end of a line used to measure water depth or vertical alignment (noun) or perfectly upright; vertical; straight up and down; or complete, absolute, and unquestionable; used only in very informal conversation (adjective) or perfectly; directly; squarely; used only in very informal conversation; or completely; absolutely; entirely; used only in very informal conversation (adverb)

The sailors had to plumb the waters to make sure the ship would not run aground in the shallows.

It was a struggle for the architect to get the weight-bearing wall plumb given the size and shape of the room.

Looking back on her past, she realized she had plumbed the depths and the heights of emotion and had lived a full life.

Since it was midnight and he didn't want to pay an extra fee, he tried to plumb the leaking pipe himself.

The plumb was lost when the line snagged on an underwater rock and snapped.

Even though they were, the walls of the haunted house didn't appear plumb due to the angles and intentionally misleading paint job.

Instead of impressing his date, his antics just made him appear a plumb idiot.

She squealed when his arrow flew plumb in the center of the bull's-eye.

He knew he was so tired after the all-nighter that his granny would have said he was "plumb worn out."

P

polyglot (PAH-lee-glot), adjective or noun
Made up of or containing more than one language; or being able to communicate fluently in many different languages (adjective) or a person who can communicate and is comfortable with several different languages (noun)

The polyglot text was helpful to students studying several languages.

The polyglot travelers always managed to communicate with someone, regardless of what country they were visiting.

The embassy was hiring extra polyglots as additional staff during the particularly heavy tourist season.

ponderous (PON-duhr-us), adjective
Clumsy and slow, often due to great weight; laborious; or unnecessarily solemn and serious; boring; emotionally tiring and weighty

The rancher's usually graceful horse was slowed under the ponderous burden of two extra riders.

By the end of the ponderous speech, even the most attentive listeners were beginning to doze and lose interest.

portent (POR-tent), noun
A sign or omen; an indication that something unusual or important, although often evil or bad luck, is about to occur

The mother of the bride refused to believe that rain on the wedding day was a portent of what was to come in the marriage.

pragmatic (prag-MA-tik), adjective
Handling things in a straightforward, logical manner; concerned only with facts; practical

He learned being pragmatic rather than becoming emotionally involved was the best way to handle business dealings.

prattle (PRAT-tuhl), verb or noun
To chatter mindlessly; pointless, superficial talk (verb) or small talk; light, unimportant conversation (noun)

The examiner let the students prattle on before the test because it seemed to calm their nerves.

Her daughter's prattle was a pleasing background for her while she cleaned up after dinner.

P

precarious (pree-CAYR-ee-uhs), adjective
Dangerously unstable; likely to fall, slip or collapse; hazardous; or dependent on unknown qualities; uncertain; shaky or questionable; or based on questionable, unproven theories or concepts

The walk down the steep slope was made more precarious by the rain that had loosened the rocks and soil.

The cyclist's lead in the race was precarious with 100 more miles to ride and his closest competitor only two minutes behind him.

Her boss was hesitant to follow her advice due to the precarious nature of the polls that had been conducted.

precedent (PRES-ih-dent), noun
A previous event that can be used as a guide for handling a current, similar event; earlier actions that can be used to justify taking similar actions in a similar situation

The office manager was concerned about the precedent she might be setting if she continued to let her assistant come into work late and leave on time.

precipitate (pree-SIP-ih-tayt), verb or (pree-SIP-ih-tiht), adjective
To fall or be thrown from a great height; or to happen quickly, usually unexpectedly and often without thought or planning; or to pour from clouds, to rain, snow, sleet, or hail (verb) or characterized by speeding ahead without caution; rushing headlong without thought or concern; or marked by acting with unnecessary and unwise haste; reckless; or unexpected, sudden, and without plan (adjective)

When the landslide hit, several houses on the coast were precipitated down the cliff and into the ocean.

The police feared a "not guilty" verdict in the latest hate crime case would precipitate a riot among the protesters.

The rain in February annoyed her because if it was going to precipitate in winter, she wanted it to snow.

The teens' precipitate race down the mountain could have ended very badly if another car had come along in the opposite direction.

The young couple realized their decision to move in together after only knowing each other a month had been precipitate.

The precipitate arrival of the king sent the household into a mad dash to prepare food and lodging for him and his retainers.

P

preclude (PREE-klood), verb

To take an action that makes something impossible; to actively prevent; or to be impossible due to a pre-existing condition

> *The club refused to preclude any child from joining because of inability to pay the fees.*

> *Her susceptibility to migraines precluded her from drinking red wine.*

precocious (PREE-coh-shus), adjective

Showing an early maturity; marked by earlier than usual mental development

> *The precocious little boy found it easier to relate to adults than to children his own age.*

Similar but Not the Same

Many words have virtually identical definitions. However, they cannot always be used in exactly the same way. Precursor (PREE-cur-ser) and predecessor (PREHD-ih-ses-ohr) are two of these words. The word precursor describes the forerunner or early model of a thing currently in use. It implies that the current model is better, more modern, or more effective than the original. Predecessor, however, is any person or thing that was previously used in the same capacity. It does not imply any evolution or growth.

---

precursor (PREE-cur-ser), noun

An event or concept that indicates what is to follow; or one that comes before; a forerunner

> *His mother secretly hoped that his earring and long black coat were not precursors to a rebellious, goth stage.*

> *The precursors to today's sleek cell phones were large and unwieldy and had very little range.*

predator (PREHD-ah-tehr), noun

A creature that hunts and feeds on other beings for its own survival; or one who destroys, hunts, hurts, or injures another, especially for selfish purposes

> *The big cats are some of the best known and fiercest predators on the planet.*

> *As a businessman, he was a predator, but as a father, husband, and friend, he was gentle, loyal, and trustworthy.*

predecessor (PREHD-ih-ses-ohr), noun
One who comes before another; the person who held the office or position
before the person now in the role; or anything that has come before the current item

*She hadn't been on the job long when she realized that her predecessor had left
behind many unfinished projects that needed to be addressed quickly.*

*The new arena is more comfortable but it doesn't have the character of its
predecessor.*

predilection (preh-dih-LEHK-shun) or (pree-dih-LEHK-shun), noun
A preference; an established liking or fondness for something

*Her small frame made it hard to believe she had a predilection for ice cream
sundaes with extra hot fudge.*

preen (PREEN), verb
To primp; to take extra care with grooming and appearance; or to clean fur
or feathers, referring to an animal's bathing; or to boast, brag or be otherwise
self-congratulatory

*The women's bathroom was full of girls taking a break from the dance floor to
preen and generally freshen up.*

The cat sat in the warm sunlight preening its thick, golden fur.

*Everyone forgave his preening because they were as excited as he was about
his recent promotion.*

presage (PREHS-ihj), noun or (PREES-ayj), verb
A warning or foretelling that something bad is going to occur; an omen
(noun) or to warn or predict something bad is going to occur (verb)

*Medieval knights considered storm clouds on the night before a battle to be a
presage of failure and possibly death.*

*She was concerned that her father's ailing health as he got older presaged an
unpleasant future.*

pretentious (PREE-ten-shus), adjective
Showy in a way that tries to impress; characterized by attempting to appear
grander, more important, or worthy of more esteem than is actually merited

*The elaborately remodeled house looked pretentious instead of elegant sur-
rounded by the more modest homes in the neighborhood.*

preternatural (pree-tuhr-NATCH-uhr-uhl) or (pree-tuhr-NATCH-ruhl), adjective
Extreme or extraordinary; far above and beyond what is normal

The characters' preternatural happiness and friendliness appealed to young children and reminded adults of an earlier, simpler time.

prevalent (PREH-veh-lent), adjective
Widespread and accepted; commonly occurring, especially at a specific time and place

The prevalent attitude throughout Hollywood was that the movie released by the young, new director was going to break box office records and send him straight to the top.

prevaricate (prih-VAYR-ih-kayt), verb
To beat around the bush; to act or speak in a manner that avoids the truth

The congressman was able to prevaricate so well that the journalists didn't realize he hadn't answered their questions until after the press conference was over.

probity (PROH-bih-tee), noun
Absolute integrity; the state of having strong principles and living by them; honor and honesty

History has painted many past leaders as men of probity, forgetting that they were also human with human flaws and failings.

proclivity (proh-KILHV-ih-tee), noun
A tendency to behave or act in a certain way

She had a proclivity toward humor that made her invaluable at the office when tensions started to run high.

procrastination (proh-cras-tih-NAY-shun), noun
The habit of putting something off until the very last minute; the act of putting off or delaying until later

She was grateful the professor gave her an incomplete in the class rather than failing her due to her procrastination in completing the final project.

prodigal (PRAH-dih-guhl), adjective or noun
Extravagant in spending habits; financially irresponsible and wasteful; or giving an impressive, generous amount; withholding nothing (adjective) or a person who spends large amounts of money frivolously and irresponsibly (noun)

The young graduate built up nearly insurmountable credit card debt with his prodigal spending habits before he realized what a mistake he was making.

Even her critics showered the mayor with prodigal praise after her handling of the threatened union strike.

Even after she had moved out on her own, the young woman continued to be such a prodigal that her father often slipped her extra cash.

prodigious (preh-DIHJ-uhs), adjective
Enormous; much larger in scope than usual; or impressive; awe-inspiring; extraordinary

He had a prodigious thirst for knowledge, so reading in the library was his favorite way to spend his spare time.

His prodigious talent brought audiences to their feet at the end of every performance.

profane (proh-FAYN), adjective or verb
Marked by cursing, inappropriate, and offensive words; or nonreligious; secular; or characterized by being insulting to religions or faith (adjective) or to treat religion or faith in an insulting and disrespectful manner (verb)

His profane humor that made him so popular in school didn't win him many friends in the business world.

The gospel singer had many religious CDs but also had a wide selection of profane music as well.

Although she was an atheist, she tried very hard not to be profane about her friends' religions and beliefs.

The young rebel had no problem spray painting the bridge but drew the line when his friends wanted to profane the church.

profligacy (PRUHF-lih-guh-see), noun
Indulgence; the tendency to spend money unwisely, generally on luxury or unnecessary items, and without regard to budget concerns

The sisters enjoyed living a life of profligacy while growing up but their parents made it clear the girls would have to make their own way once they were adults.

profuse (proh-FYOOS), adjective
Given in large amounts; handed out freely, with little reservation
The paper was so profuse in its compliments of even mediocre achievements that praise from the editors didn't mean much.

proliferation (proh-LIHF-eh-ray-shun), noun
Rapid growth or increase in numbers, parts, or aspects
The proliferation of the earth's population has long been a concern of both scientists and environmentalists.

prolific (proh-LIHF-ik), adjective
Creating large numbers of works or results; or reproducing in large quantities
The prolific author could write up to three novels in a single year.
It was the gardener's hope that his plants would be prolific so the entire area would be green within just a few seasons.

prolix (PROH-liks) or (proh-LIKS), adjective
Excessively long or wordy, used when describing writings or a speech
The challenge of writing a study guide is to make it long enough to be useful but not prolix.

propensity (proh-PEN-sih-tee), noun
Having a natural tendency to behave in a certain way
He had a propensity toward messiness that he knew he would have to get over.

propitious (proh-PIH-shus), adjective
Presenting a strong chance of success; favorable; appearing to be lucky
The man found it propitious that on the day he had finally gotten up his nerve to ask the woman out, she was sitting in the break room by herself.

prosaic (proh-ZAY-ik), adjective
Plain, straightforward, and easy to understand; not flowery or poetic; or dull, boring, and unimaginative
The professor encouraged his students to be prosaic in their papers because he knew that having a clear writing style would serve them well in later life.
The actor's prosaic interpretation of one of the most emotionally moving monologues ever written made the casting agents cringe.

proscribe (proh-SRIYB), verb
To prohibit, ban, or forbid; or to declare illegal or immoral; to openly condemn

The director of the children's program decided to proscribe smoking anywhere on the grounds so the staff wouldn't give the kids a bad impression.

Many nations joined together to proscribe the crimes the rebels had committed during the civil war in their country.

prosperity (pruh-SPAR-ih-tee), noun
The state of being financially well-off; financially successful and comfortable

Many people leave their homelands and come to the United States hoping to find prosperity and a better life.

protuberant (proh-TOO-buh-rant) or (proh-TYOO-buh-rant) or (preh-TOO-buh-rant), adjective
Sticking out; bulging; swollen out

The carnival mirror gave his nose a large, protuberant look.

provident (PRAH-vih-dent), adjective
Making financial arrangements for the future; planning for and thinking about the future

Her grandfather was provident enough to set up a savings account on her first birthday to pay for her college education.

provincial (proh-VIN-shul), adjective
Unsophisticated; not terribly educated; unworldly; may imply narrow mindedness or a certain degree of naivety

After living in the city for a year, she came to realize how provincial some of her attitudes had always been.

provocative (preh-VAHK-ah-tihv), adjective
Marked by an ability to excite, intrigue, or cause a reaction, usually intentionally; or intended to arouse sexually

The provocative editorial calling for the resignation of the chief of police caused outrage among his supporters.

The provocative blouse really wasn't her style but her friends had assured her it was still appropriate.

proximity (prok-SIM-ih-tee), noun
Closeness or nearness, either in time or actual distance; next to
Even though the young man was usually quite composed, he always became clumsy and flustered whenever the young woman was in close proximity to him.

prudence (PROO-dens), noun
The act of showing care and being concerned for the future; discretion; the ability to act in a way to avoid embarrassment, discomfort, or awkward situations
She suspected she would go into politics one day so she acted with prudence even when her friends were throwing caution to the wind.

punctilious (punk-TIL-ee-uhs), adjective
Very aware of the rules of conduct or etiquette; knowledgeable of every small detail
His grandmother was punctilious and had insisted upon perfect table manners, even when he and his brother had been children.

pungent (PUHN-jent), adjective
Marked by a sharp, strong, or even bitter taste or smell; or penetrating; nearly viciously to the point; sharp
The neighbors were first alerted to the fire when the pungent smell of smoke drifted from one apartment into the next.
Although she could be gracious and warm, she also had a reputation for making pungent remarks if anyone took advantage of her kindness.

pusillanimous (pyoo-sih-LAN-ih-mus), adjective
Cowardly; lacking courage; fearful or spineless
The students' pusillanimous whining when told they would be handling live reptiles annoyed the teacher even though she expected it.

putrefy (PYOO-trih-fiy), verb
To rot and produce a foul odor; to decay and smell bad
The family froze the chicken bones left over from dinner so they wouldn't putrefy before the trash went out later in the week.

pyre (PIYR), noun
A pile of wood, twigs, and other flammable material, usually used to burn a corpse as part of a funeral ritual
Even the guys choked up during the scene in the movie in which the hero lit the pyre for the heroine's funeral.

quaff (KWAHF), verb
To drink deeply with great gusto and enjoyment, usually an alcoholic beverage
Oktoberfest is a traditional time to find friends laughing and quaffing ale while toasting each other's health.

qualm (KWALM), noun
A feeling of uneasiness; a feeling of doubt, worry, or concern
The woman's adventurous spirit allowed her to take great risks without the slightest qualm.

quandary (KWAHN-duh-ree) or (KWAHN-dree), noun
A state of confusion or uncertainty about how to handle a difficult situation; a dilemma
He found himself in a quandary when offered a job with a new company and a promotion from his current employer.

quell (KWEL), verb
To put an end to, often by the use of or threat of force; to force to stop; or to silence or subdue; or to ease; to calm; to make quiet
The military was able to quell the rebels before the resistance could gain a foothold and become bloody.
One look from the headmaster was enough to quell any thoughts the students might have had about making excuses or trying to get out of being punished.
If a child has been traumatized in some way, it becomes harder to quell even their irrational fears.

query (KWIHR-ee), noun or verb

A question or inquiry, generally used in formal situations (noun) or to ask a question, especially when expressing a doubt or concern; to request a clarification (verb)

The press corps had to present their queries about the new policy in advance to the prime minister's staff.

The thesis review board queried the candidate on many of the more unconventional and challenging aspects of the theories presented in her paper.

quibble (KWIH-bul), noun or verb

A minor objection or criticism, especially over a trivial matter (noun) or to find fault through nitpicking (verb)

The few quibbles brought up by the pickiest judge were not enough to drop the skater's score in the competition.

The coupled quibbled over many things but they were really deeply in love and both knew it.

quiescent (kwee-EH-sehnt), adjective

Marked by inactivity; being in a period of rest, usually temporary

The lab would seem quiescent for months at a time then there would be a flurry of activity as a new breakthrough was discovered.

quotidian (kwoh-TIH-dee-ahn), adjective

Everyday, ordinary, or commonplace

After having been away from home for so long, she found pleasure in even the most quotidian activities of daily life.

raconteur (rak-uhn-TUHR), noun

An excellent storyteller; one who tells amusing and interesting stories

He was such a gifted raconteur he managed to make even the most ordinary events sound lively and interesting.

ramify (RAM-ih-fiy), verb

To have or cause complications; to cause further difficulties to develop

The steps the group first took to repair the problem only seemed to ramify the situation further.

rancor (rang-KOR), noun

Long-standing anger; bitterness, especially when held and nurtured over time

None of her friends understood why she still spoke with such rancor about an event that had happened when they were all still in school.

rapacious (ruh-PAY-shus), adjective

Greedy in an aggressive way; wanting more than one's fair share

In his will, the old man left everything to his servants and a few close friends because he was too aware of the rapacious nature of his family.

rarefy or **rarify** (RAER-eh-fiy), verb

To become thin; to make less dense; to weaken; or to have less oxygen than the norm, generally used to describe air at high altitudes

Women should be sure to take calcium as they age so that their bones do not rarefy and become brittle.

As the mountaineers climbed higher, the air began to rarefy, making it more difficult to breathe.

How Do You Spell That?

Most words have one spelling. However, every rule has exceptions. Rarefy is one of those exceptions. While the most common spelling is r-a-r-e-f-y, it is sometimes spelled r-a-r-i-f-y. They are both pronounced (RAER-eh-fiy.) Use the most common spelling should you choose to write the word. Just know that, if you see it spelled with an i, it is the same word and still spelled correctly.

raucous (RAW-kuhs), adjective

Loud and unruly; rowdy; disruptive and noisy

The neighbors were generally patient with the raucous parties thrown by the fraternity but sometimes called the police when things got too out of hand.

raze (RAYZ), verb

To flatten; to completely destroy; to tear down to the ground

The town council decided to raze the run-down city hall and build a modern one on the same site.

reactionary (ree-AK-shun-ayr-ee), adjective or noun
Marked by opposing liberal political and social views; characterized by being
against reform (adjective) or a person who holds very conservative views and
beliefs (noun)

Most news talk show hosts are either so liberal or so reactionary that the pro-
grams turn into nothing more than shouting matches.

She enjoyed her reputation as the only reactionary on a campus of bleeding
heart liberals.

rebuff (ree-BUF), noun or verb
A deliberately cold and abrupt rejection or refusal (noun) or to reject in a
particularly cold or unfeeling way; or to push back; to repel (verb)

Although he hadn't expected to be granted an interview, he didn't think the
secretary should have given him such a harsh rebuff.

She tried to be subtle but eventually had to rebuff his advances.

The defense managed to rebuff the opposing team's final effort to make a score-
tying goal.

rebuttal (rih-BUHT-tuhl), noun
A statement or speech given to contradict or answer a statement or speech
that has come before it

The State of the Union Address is always immediately followed by a short
rebuttal made by a ranking member of the minority party.

recant (ree-KANT), verb
To take back a statement; to vow one no longer believes a specific opinion or
idea previously believed, generally made under pressure

In the 1600s and 1700s, many scientists whose discoveries challenged the
Church were forced to recant their findings or else face death.

reciprocal (ree-sih-PROH-cul), adjective
Given in return; exchanged; felt or performed by each side

Although the generals were on opposing sides of the war, they had developed a
reciprocal admiration for the other's skill.

reciprocity (res-ih-PRAH-sih-tee), noun
The practice of exchanging goods, services, or ideals with another for mutual benefit; an exchange in which both parties gain
The couple said the reason they had stayed together for so long was they had a marriage of reciprocity, love, and respect.

recondite (reh-KON-diyt) or (rih-KON-diyt), adjective
Difficult to understand; outside of common knowledge; or hidden; out of view; concealed
The New York Times crossword puzzle is recognized as one of the most challenging and recondite of any word puzzles.
She hoped her dissertation would address some recondite, undiscovered aspect of her field that would bring her acclaim.

recrudescent (ree-KROO-dih-sent), adjective
To start up again; to reoccur after a period of being dormant; to come out of remission
The brief truce hadn't made the recrudescent hostilities any less violent.

rectify (REK-tih-fiy), verb
To set straight or make right; to make amends by correcting the situation
He knew he had hurt his sister badly enough that a simple apology was not going to rectify the matter.

redoubtable (rih-DOW-tuh-bul), adjective
Instilling fear or respect; causing awe; or worthy of respect and recognition
He used his redoubtable reputation in the military to gain a political appointment in civilian life.
Thomas Jefferson's redoubtable words declaring independence from Britain still have the power to move people the first time they read them.

redress (rih-DREHS), verb or noun
To remedy or make right; to make amends for or to (verb) or compensation; a remedy for a wrong done (noun)
The company promised to redress the customer's complaints.
The jury was able to give the man financial redress but it could never restore the emotional peace he had lost to the crime.

R

refractory (rih-FRAK-tih-ree), adjective
Openly and stubbornly resistant to authority or control; or resistant to heat .
or other stimulus; or difficult to treat, referring to a medical condition
> *In the 1960s and 1970s, any time large groups formed to listen to a passion-*
> *ate speaker, there was always the concern the situation would change from peaceful*
> *gathering to refractory mob.*
>
> *Refractory glass is ideal for use in cooking because it will not break when*
> *exposed to high temperatures.*
>
> *Her acne proved refractory enough she finally went to a dermatologist.*

refulgent (rih-FUHL-jent) or (rih-FOOL-jent), adjective
Shining brightly; as if lit by the sun
> *The young mother had a refulgent glow that lasted throughout her pregnancy.*

refute (ree-FYOOT), verb
To prove false or incorrect; to present opposing facts
> *The adventures he claimed to have always took place when he was alone so, as*
> *unbelievable as they seemed, no one could ever refute them.*

regicide (REH-jih-siyd), noun
The intentional killing of a king; murder or assassination of a king
> *Historically, regicide was a risky if effective way for a pretender to the throne*
> *to take over the monarchy.*

reiterate (ree-IH-tuhr-ayt), verb
To repeat something, usually for clarification or emphasis
> *The professor's policy was never to reiterate instructions.*

relegate (rehl-uh-GAYT), verb
To refer to another; to pass off responsibility for; or to demote; to lower in
rank or responsibility; or to banish or expel; to put in an obscure or out of
the way place
> *One of the joys of being CEO was that she could relegate the minor tasks she*
> *hated.*
>
> *The police officer was relegated to desk work until he completely healed from*
> *the fall he took on the ice.*
>
> *The ugly sculpture from her aunt was relegated to the dusty top of a bookshelf.*

R

remonstrate (ree-MON-strayt) or (reh-MUHN-strayt), verb
To forcefully protest; to argue against
Although she was the only person to remonstrate the action, several people in the meeting voted against it.

remorse (rih-MORS), noun
Deep regret or guilt for actions taken in the past
The jury gave the young man the lightest sentence possible because he showed such obvious and sincere remorse for his behavior.

renege (rih-NIHG) or (rih-NEHG), verb
To go back on a promise; to fail to keep a commitment
The director was left in a bind when his financial backers reneged on their contract to fund the shoot.

renounce (RIH-nowns) or (REE-nowns), verb
To formally give up on a claim, title, or position; or to refuse to support any further; to deny or refuse to obey any longer
The prince shocked the world when he renounced his claim to the throne in order to enter the priesthood.

The Civil War began when the southern states renounced the authority the United States had over them and seceded from the nation.

repast (rih-PAST), noun
A meal
The poor man's repast may have been small but it was made with love and shared willingly.

repine (rih-PIYN), verb
To complain; to be discontented; to express dissatisfaction; or to long for; to miss
The woman seemed determine to repine about everything at the resort from the food to the weather in spite of the fact that everyone else was enjoying it.

Usually she enjoyed living in California but in autumn she repined for her childhood home in New England.

reprehensible (rep-rhee-HENS-ih-bul), adjective

Truly disgusting or deplorable; deserving of scorn

Some people believe the death penalty is a reprehensible abuse of power while others believe it deters crime and provides the victims some justice.

reprove (rih-PROOV), verb

To reprimand or scold; to express displeasure

The principal reproved the students he caught under the stairwell cutting classes.

repudiate (rih-PYOO-dee-ayt), verb

To claim as invalid; to reject as being valid; or to vigorously deny as having any truth; to state something is completely false

Since the couple was married by a justice of the peace, the bride's mother repudiated the union until it had been blessed by a priest.

He repudiated the accusations against him long before the investigation proved he was not involved in the situation.

Similar but Not the Same

Many words have similar meanings but are used in different contexts. This is the case for renounce (RIH-nowns) or (REE-nowns) and repudiate (rih-PYOO-dee-ayt). To renounce something is to state it no longer has power or control, meaning it once did. On the other hand, to repudiate something is to claim it is and always has been false. To renounce is to reject as false now. To repudiate is to reject as false always.

requisite (REH-kwih-zit), adjective or noun

Necessary; required; vital (adjective) or that which is required; something essential (noun)

In order to lose weight, a person must take the requisite steps of eating well and exercising.

The requisites for the job included phone skills, a basic understanding of data entry, and attention to detail.

R

requite (rih-KWIYT), verb

To repay, as a debt; or to return an emotion; to feel the same way

The candidate knew she could never completely requite all the debts she owed the people who had helped get her nominated.

His heart leapt when he realized the young woman did indeed requite his feelings for her.

What I Meant to Say Was . . .

Words that are spelled similarly can cause confusion if you read too quickly. Requisite (REH-kwih-zit) and requite (rih-KWIYT) are close but not the same. A requisite is something that is required or vital, but to requite means to return feelings or pay back.

---

rescind (rih-SIHND), verb

To take back; to make void; to negate

The man's driver's license was rescinded after he was convicted.

resilient (rih-ZIHL-yehnt), adjective

Able to bounce back after a problem or difficulty; unbroken emotionally and spiritually; or springy; able to reshape after being squeezed or misshapen

Her friends were not too concerned about her when she lost the job because they knew how resilient she had always been.

The toy was resilient enough to withstand even a toddler's attention.

resolution (rehz-uh-LOO-shun), noun

Firm, unwavering determination; or a decision to do something; or the clarity or detail that can be seen in an electronically produced image; or the part of a book, movie, or story in which the plot is wrapped up; or an act or official suggestion presented to an official, voting body

Her resolution to be the first in her family to attend college drove her to study harder and more often than most of her peers.

Most people make at least one resolution at the beginning of every new year.

The resolution to the book was unsatisfying considering how much the readers had come to care about the characters.

The board could not vote on the resolution before it until a majority of the members were in attendance.

R

resonance (REHZ-eh-nehns), noun

The quality of being resounding or having great meaning; or deep, rich tones

The resonance of President Roosevelt's words during World War II uplifted an entire nation and helped the world stay strong during a dark, frightening time.

The resonance of the church bells rang out over the city.

resplendent (reh-SPLEND-ehnt), adjective

Unusually beautiful and dazzling; decorated in a breathtaking way

The cathedral was impressive at any time but when lit by the sunset it was resplendent and awe-inspiring.

restrained (rhih-STRAYND), adjective or verb

Marked by emotional control or a cool manner; dispassionate (adjective) or held in place; physically controlled; kept from freedom of movement (verb)

His restrained manner made him appear indifferent, but he was simply very professional and knew when to control his emotions.

The dog was restrained by his leash and the tall fence but the mail carrier still didn't like the look of its teeth.

retinue (RHEH-tih-noo), noun

The group of employees accompanying an important person

The singer required rooms for herself and her entire retinue.

retract (rih-TRAKT), verb

To draw back in; to pull back; or to take back a statement

Once the puppy left her alone, the cat relaxed, retracted its claws, and went to sleep in the sun.

When he saw the shock on the young woman's face, he wished he could retract the invitation but was grateful he hadn't when she accepted.

reverence (REH-ver-uhns), noun

A deep, loving respect or awe; great admiration combined with love; or an act that shows respect, often a bow or curtsy

The reverence shown the old king was testament to what a fair and benevolent ruler he had always been.

The visitors kissed the cardinal's ring in reverence as they entered the room before getting on with the interview.

reverent (REHV-er-ehnt), adjective
Characterized by showing respect; worthy of admiration
It is appropriate to maintain a reverent silence in all places of worship, regardless of your own beliefs.

rigor (RHIH-gehr), noun
Something hard to live through or manage; difficulty; difficult to endure; or strictness; extreme hardship
Many southerners who move north soon discover they are not cut out for the rigor of even one winter in Montana.
The rigors of boot camp are meant to weed out people who cannot handle the trials of combat.

risible (RIZ-uh-bul), adjective
Funny or amusing; worthy of laughter
The risible antics of him as a baby with the puppy made him wish his mother had never gotten a video camera.

robust (ROH-bust) or (roh-BUST), adjective
Healthy, vigorous; or strong; well-built; able to withstand stress; or characterized by fullness and depth; hearty
The trainer's robust health made her an inspiration to everyone in the gym, not just her own clients.
The robust wrestler was willing to take on all challengers who thought they could go three minutes with him.
The robust laughter coming from the basement assured her the men were having a good time shooting pool and watching the game.

rotund (roh-TUND), adjective
Plump or chubby; curvy; referring to a person; or round; shaped as a sphere or orb; referring to an item or structure
His full beard, jolly laugh and rotund tummy made him a perfect man to play Santa Claus in the parade.
The cook stacked the pots in the cupboard because they were too rotund to fit on the shelves.

ruffian (RUF-ee-uhn) or (RUF-yuhn), noun
A person who is tough and disorderly, particularly one who commits a crime
The store owner knew the teens were just bored kids, not ruffians, so he let them hang out in the parking lot after school.

sage (SAYJ), noun or adjective
A wise person, usually implies wisdom gained from age (noun) or characterized by a sense of calm and great wisdom (adjective)
The old woman was considered a sage within the small community.
As a teenager, he had always rebelled against his grandparents' sage advice but longed for it once he was an adult.

> ### Don't I Know That Word?
> Sometimes you may know only the most common definition of a word. Sage (SAYJ) may be one of those words. You know that sage is a shade of green. If you cook, you may know that sage is also a spice. However, if you double-check the listing in the book, you'll discover it is also a very wise person or an adjective indicating the presence of great wisdom.

salacious (suh-LAY-shus), adjective
Having to do with lust or sexual desire; bawdy; dealing with sexual matters in an indecent way
She preferred to work out at home so she didn't have to deal with the salacious looks that followed her when she was at the gym.

salient (SAY-lee-ehnt) or (SAY-lyent), adjective
The most important or striking aspect; the part that demands the most attention
Part of the attorney's job was to keep the jurors from being distracted away from the salient points of the case.

salubrious (sa-LOO-bree-uhs), adjective
Promoting or encouraging health and well-being
The couple realized that the occasional weekend away from the demands of their jobs and children had a salubrious effect on their relationship.

salutary (SAL-yeh-tayr-ree), adjective
Intending to be helpful or to repair a situation; healing; having a good result
Taking a salutary soak in the hot springs may not cure every physical condition as once believed, but it is very good for curing stress-related ones.

sanction (SANG-shun), verb
To give formal or official approval; or to punish with the intent of changing a behavior, generally on a national or international level
The family of the great actor convinced him to sanction a biography while he could still be interviewed directly.
The United Nations will sanction countries that don't abide by international treaties or law.

sardonic (sar-DON-ik), adjective
Cynically ironic; bitterly humorous
Her sardonic smile didn't quite hide her disappointment at being the last one cut from the competition.

satiate (SAY-shee-ayt), verb
To satisfy completely; to want or need no more of a longing or appetite
The enormous library held enough books to satiate even the most enthusiastic reader.

saturate (saht-CHUR-ayt), verb
To drench with a liquid until no more can be held; to soak completely; to totally fill
The trick to growing basil from a seed is to saturate the soil when the seed is first planted and then keep it very moist thereafter.

satyr (SAY-ter), or (SAH-ter), noun
A character from Greek mythology with the torso and head of a man but the ears, legs, and horns of a goat, known for enjoying self-indulgent celebrations
Pan, a Greek character who loved mischief and troublemaking, is often drawn or sculpted to appear as a satyr.

savor (SAY-vor), verb

To enjoy completely; to appreciate with great gusto; often referring to the flavor of food

The historian was determined to savor every moment, sight, and sound during her first visit to Washington, D.C.

savory (SAY-vuh-ree), adjective

A spicy, rather than sweet, flavoring; or morally pure; uncorrupted

The savory meat pie was delicious and complemented the creamy sweet potatoes perfectly on a cold winter night.

When the judge's less-than-savory past became public, he withdrew from the nomination process to save himself and the president further embarrassment.

Watch Out!

It seems obvious that sweet and sweetly are related words. But look out for words that look related but really aren't. Savor and savory appear to be different forms of the same word, but they really are not. Savor (SAY-vor) means to appreciate greatly. Savory (SAY-vuh-ree) means either a spicy flavoring or pure and innocent.

scabbard (SKA-burd), noun

The sheath or holder for a knife or sword, usually made of steel or leather

The pirate withdrew his sword from its scabbard with an ease that indicated great experience in dueling.

scanty (SKAN-tee), adjective

Small to the point of being barely useful; less than is needed; barely adequate

Her scanty paycheck was barely enough to cover her monthly expenses, but it was worth it to live in the city she loved.

scintilla (sin-TIHL-lah), adjective

A tiny amount or a trace; a quick flash

The scintilla of fear that shuddered through her when the power appeared to be out disappeared when the lights came on and her friends yelled, "Surprise!"

scrupulous (SKROO-pyoo-lus), adjective
Having great attention to detail; thorough and attentive; or highly moral; concerned with behaving well
 The students took scrupulous notes knowing they could learn as much from the guest lecturer as they could any of their full-time professors.
 Even when their relationship was rocky, he was too scrupulous to even think about having an affair.

seclusion (seh-KLOO-shun), noun
The state of being away from other people; being in an exceedingly private place
 The writer found it helpful to go into seclusion the last month before an approaching deadline with her publisher.

sedentary (SEHD-ehn-tayr-ee), adjective
Inactive; characterized by sitting often and not getting much exercise
 He discovered he was gaining weight once he took a sedentary job after being a camp counselor for so long.

sedition (seh-DIH-shun), noun
Actions or words that encourage rebellion against a government; the act of trying to motivate people to overthrow the government
 While complaining about the government is protected by the right of free speech, actual sedition is not protected.

sedulous (SED-jel-lus), adjective
Characterized by constant and diligent care and concern
 She was willing to relax her sedulous attempts to lose weight while they were on the cruise because she knew she would be diligent again at the end of the week.

servile (SER-viyl), adjective
Willing to serve others; most comfortable when serving another in a lesser or submissive role
 The feminist movement grew from women wanting to be more than just servile homemakers.

150   severance

S

severance (SEHV-er-ans) or (SEHV-rans), noun

The separation of parties or parts

> *The severance of the smaller movie studio from its larger parent company was a shock to everyone who followed the film industry.*

shard (SHARD), noun

A piece of broken glass, pottery, metal, or other breakable material, usually having sharp edges

> *The shards from the broken glass scattered across the kitchen floor, making it treacherous for anyone in bare feet.*

sinecure (SIYN-ih-kyoor) or (SIHN-ih-kyoor), noun

A job that requires very little work but that offers a paycheck and other benefits

> *He needed a position that was basically a sinecure so he would have time to study while he was at the office in order to keep his grades up.*

sinuous (SIN-yoo-uhs), adjective

Curvy; characterized by having many turns and twists; or graceful and smooth

> *The sinuous road through the mountains was more dangerous than ever after the ice storm.*
>
> *The cat's sinuous speed allowed it to outmaneuver the gangly puppy with ease.*

How Do You Spell That?

Think you know how to spell a word? Some words have multiple correct spellings. Skeptic is one of them. While the most common spelling is s-k-e-p-t-i-c, it is sometimes spelled s-c-e-p-t-i-c. They are both pronounced (SKEP-tik). Use the most common spelling when you write the word. But know that if you see it spelled with a c, it is the same word and it is spelled correctly.

skeptic (SKEHP-tik), noun

A person who automatically doubts the truth about ideas, concepts, or beliefs commonly accepted by others

> *She was such a skeptic that she rarely believed in anything she couldn't see or touch, regardless of how strong an argument someone made in favor of the concept.*

skiff (SKIF), noun
A certain kind of small boat propelled by oar, sail, or motor, usually with a flat bottom
A skiff was available during summer to take tourists from one side of the lake to the other.

sluggard (SLUH-gehrd), noun
An overall lazy person, has negative connotations
He was so busy that his wife often reminded him that spending one afternoon relaxing would not turn him into a sluggard.

sluggish (SLUH-gish), adjective
Slow moving; slow to respond; having a lack of energy
The August day was so hot and lazy that even the river behind the house seemed sluggish.

solace (SOH-luhs), noun
Comfort in difficult or trying times; ease from pain
After her grandfather died, she found solace in the company of others who had loved him.

solicitous (soh-LIHS-ih-tus), adjective
Marked by being concerned; characterized by offering care and attention
She knew her friend was trying to be helpful while she was sick, but his solicitous nature was beginning to get on her nerves.

solvent (SAWL-vent), adjective
Having enough money to meet all financial obligations; being able to pay one's debts
He worked very hard to pay off all his loans after college and planned to stay solvent from then on out.

somniferous (sahm-NIF-her-uhs), adjective
Bringing on sleep or tiredness
Hot cocoa always had a somniferous effect on her, so it was her favorite late night drink when she couldn't sleep.

somnolent (SAHM-nuh-lent), adjective
Drowsy, sleepy, or lazy in a tired way
The baby fell asleep on her father's chest listening to the somnolent tones of his voice as he whispered to her.

Similar but Not the Same

Many words may seem synonymous, but subtle differences in meaning mean they cannot be used interchangeably. Somniferous (sahm-NIF-her-uhs) and somnolent (SAHM-nuh-lent) are two of these words. Something that is somniferous will bring on sleep or cause tiredness, whereas something that is somnolent is already sleepy and drowsy.

---

sonorous (saw-NUH-rus) or (SAW-nuh-rus) or (SOH-nuh-rus), adjective
Impressively deep, rich, and full, generally referring to a sound
His sonorous bass voice made him perfect to play the villain in the movie.

sophistry (SOF-ih-stree), noun
An intentionally misleading and false argument or claim used to misrepresent
Most people in the office were accustomed to his sophistry so it was more difficult for him to get the projects he wanted.

soporific (sah-POR-if-ik) or (soh-POR-if-ik), adjective or noun
Tending to bring about sleep; sleepy (adjective) or a product or substance that brings about sleepiness (noun)
Riding in the car had a soporific effect on the baby, so her parents drove her around the block when she wouldn't go to sleep.
The medicine was great for her headaches but it was also a soporific, so she could only take it at night.

specious (SPEE-shus), adjective
Reasonable at first glance but actually false; believable on the surface but not true; plausible but incorrect
Part of the professor's job was to point out the specious logic in her students' arguments and help them find the truth of the situation.

spurn (SPERN), verb

To reject in a cold and rude manner

She pretended to spurn the girls getting ready for the dance but in reality she was just hurt because no one had asked her to go.

squalid (SKWAH-lihd), adjective

Disgustingly dirty; grimy and practically unlivable; or completely without morals or standards

The neighborhood had once been a squalid, dangerous part of town but the current residents had worked hard to make a decent place to live and raise a family.

The new CEO put an end to the squalid business practices his predecessor had developed and encouraged.

stagnation (stag-NAY-shun), noun

A period of time without growth; the state of not moving forward; often referring to an economic condition

The mountain village decided to turn itself into a tourist attraction to break the stagnation that had settled there since the last mine closed.

stigma (STIG-mah), noun

A mark of shame or embarrassment; something considered appropriate to hide

There is still such a stigma associated with counseling and therapy that many people are not getting the care they need because they don't want to be seen as crazy.

stoic (STOH-ik), adjective or noun

Showing no expression; apparently immune to pain, hurt, or other emotion (adjective) or a person who shows little or no emotion regardless of the situation (noun)

She was so stoic at the funeral that even her sister thought she was unaffected by their grandmother's death.

Although strangers thought he was a stoic, his friends knew he was actually quite warm and open once he was comfortable in a situation.

stolid (STAH-luhd), adjective

Exceedingly calm; rarely emotionally out of control; dependable and unexcitable

Her stolid presence was a blessing for the children who were confused by the other adults' reaction to the crisis.

strident (STRIY-dent), adjective

Obnoxiously and often unnecessarily loud

His strident objections to the plane's delay tried the gate attendant's patience.

stupefy (STOO-pih-fiy), verb

To make a person unable to think clearly; to stun; to dull the senses; or to amaze, shock, and astonish

The teacher's lectures were so boring they managed to stupefy all but the most attentive students.

His parents were stupefied by his decision to take a year traveling around Europe instead of accepting the scholarship offered him by the university.

stymie (STIY-mee), verb

To confuse to the point of being unable to figure out the situation; to stop or halt progress

The construction of the bookshelf was stymied when he accidentally dropped the screws behind the couch.

subordinate (suh-BOR-dih-nuht), adjective or noun or (sub-BOR-dih-nayt), verb

Considered less important; secondary; lower in the hierarchy (adjective) or a person who is below another in rank or position (noun) or to make something or someone lower in importance than something or someone else (verb)

He was unwilling to take a position that was subordinate to the one he had previously held.

She was well-liked as a supervisor because she treated her subordinates professionally and with respect.

In modern relationships, the women do not need to subordinate their desires to men's.

subpoena (suh-PEE-nah), noun or verb

An order requiring a person to appear in court to testify (noun) or to order a person to appear in court to testify (verb)

After witnessing the accident, she received a subpoena to give her version of events.

The lawyer didn't want to subpoena the child if there was any way to avoid it.

Which Word?

Many words can be used as a noun, an adjective, or a verb. Subordinate is one of them. When used as a noun or an adjective, it is pronounced suh-BOR-dih-nuht. The noun subordinate is a person of lower rank or standing than someone else. The adjective subordinate indicates a lower rank or standing. When used as a verb, it is pronounced sub-BOR-dih-nayt. The verb to subordinate means to make something or someone less important than something else. Ready for a fun sentence? The president's immediate subordinate was only subordinate to the president, so his wishes were rarely subordinated to anyone else's wishes. Read closely so you don't confuse the parts of speech!

---

subside (suhb-SIYD), verb

To lower to normal or almost normal levels; to decrease; to ease off

The doctors told her she could not work out until two weeks after the pain in her broken foot had subsided.

substantiate (suhb-STAN-shee-ayt), verb

To confirm; to give proof of presented or presumed facts

The students had to substantiate every claim they made in their research papers.

subterfuge (SUB-tehr-fyooj), noun

A plan or strategy developed to mislead or trick

It took an elaborate subterfuge and the assistance of several of her friends to pull off the surprise birthday party.

sumptuous (sum-CHYOO-uhs), adjective
Large and elegant enough to indicate great time or expense; splendid
The reception included a sumptuous spread of delicacies and fine wines.

supercilious (soo-per-SIL-ee-uhs), adjective
Acting as if one is better than others; snobby
The supercilious girl ended up feeling foolish when she realized the young woman she had ignored was the daughter of a famous rock star.

superfluous (soo-PER-floo-us), adjective
Unnecessary; extra; more than enough
Since her walls were already covered in posters, buying another one seemed superfluous.

supernumerary (soo-per-NOO-muh-ruh-ree) or (soo-per-NYOO-muh-ruh-ree), adjective
Extra and not necessary; more than the usual amount; excessive
The coach was always grateful when he had a supernumerary number of hopefuls try out because it meant he could be picky about his team and not have settle for poor players.

supersede (soo-pehr-SEED), verb
Take the place of; replace; or to override or overrule
The SUV has superseded the minivan as the choice for large families who need a roomy vehicle.
The boss' ideas superseded all other suggestions, regardless of how valid they were.

supine (soo-PIYN) or (SOO-piyn), adjective
Having one's face up; lying on the back, face up; or showing lack of care, concern or resistance in the face of injustice or wrongdoing
After her knee surgery, she could only lay supine until the doctors took her out of traction.
The field workers found the residents of the neighborhood frustratingly supine considering the crime rates in the area.

supplant (suh-PLANT), verb
To replace; to take the place of and perform the same function of another
The United Nations' goal was to supplant the dictatorship with a democratic government on the small island.

supplicate (SUP-lih-cayt), verb
To ask humbly for something; to plead with great earnestness
The people at the vigil took a moment of silence to supplicate God for the health and safety of the men and women serving in the military.

surcharge (SUHR-charj), noun
An additional charge above and beyond the price or original amount
He was going to get cash from the ATM but decided the $2 surcharge was too much to pay just to have some extra money in his pocket.

surfeit (SUHR-fit), adjective
An extra amount; more than is necessary
Although she knew she would have a surfeit of food at the party, she thought it was better to have leftovers than have people leave hungry.

sybarite (SIY-ber-iyt), noun
A person devoted to luxury; one who is self-indulgent when it comes to pleasure and living well
Having grown up without any money at all, the wealthy actress quickly developed a reputation for being a sybarite.

synthesis (SIN-thih-sihs), noun
The combining of two or more individual parts to create a new whole
The synthesis of his charm and her intelligence made them an almost unbeatable debate team.

taciturn (TAS-ih-tern), adjective
Quiet or uncommunicative; not given to talking or making conversation
Her taciturn uncle was embarrassed but flattered when asked to make a toast at the wedding.

tantamount (TANT-uh-mownt), adjective
Being equal to in importance or seriousness; being as good as
> *For the young actor, the award nomination was tantamount to a declaration that he had succeeded in achieving his life's dream.*

temerity (tuh-MEHR-ih-tee), noun
Fearless self-confidence; bravery and courage
> *Her temerity allowed her to march into the dean's office and hand him her application in person.*

tentative (TENT-ah-tive), adjective
Not completely set or agreed upon; still subject to change; or shy; timid; hesitant
> *She was not sure what time the meeting would end, so they made tentative plans to meet at eight o'clock.*
> *The baby's first, tentative steps made his parents cheer so loudly she got scared and lost her balance.*

tenuous (TEN-yoo-uhs), adjective
Weak, slight, and liable to break
> *The loose button on her coat was being held by one last tenuous thread so she knew she needed to repair it or risk losing the button.*

terrestrial (tehr-RES-tree-uhl), adjective
Having to do with the earth or land
> *Although polar bears are mostly terrestrial, they are also very comfortable in the water.*

terse (TERS), adjective
Short and to the point; abrupt; brief, may imply an unwillingness to speak
> *When he was angry, he answers to questions became terse and sarcastic.*

timorous (TIM-er-us), adjective
Nervous and hesitant; showing a lack of confidence or courage
> *The young singer's voice was timorous in front of the audience until she relaxed and got into the song.*

torpid (TOR-pid), adjective

Slow, lacking energy or enthusiasm; inactive and lazy

The oppressive heat made even the dogs torpid, lying in the shade, tongues lolling.

torpor (TOR-pur), noun

The state of being tired, lazy, or inactive; apathy or indifference

The torpor that settled over the offices when the candidate appeared to be losing couldn't be shaken even by a slight rise in the polls.

torque (TORK), verb

To twist; to apply pressure causing a turn or rotation

The football player torqued his knee badly enough that he left the game, but not badly enough to cause serious damage to the ligaments.

torrid (TOR-ihd), adjective

Scorching hot; overheated; parched; or passionate and fiery; or energetic to the point of frenzy

Traveling through the torrid desert sands takes care and preparation or it can be a dangerous journey.

Their torrid love affair evolved into a marriage that lasted over fifty years.

The torrid activity at the hotel before the arrival of the prime minister was well masked by a calm and professional lobby staff.

tout (TOUT), verb

To praise highly, usually hoping to convince of worth or even to sell

She touted the benefits of yoga for overall health so often that her friends finally tried it in spite of being skeptical.

tractable (TRAKT-ah-bul), adjective

Controlled or managed easily, referring to a being or a situation

The puppy became far more tractable after six weeks of obedience school.

transient (TRAN-zee-ent), adjective or noun
Fleeting or temporary; passing with time; or staying in one place for a short period of time before moving on (adjective) or a person who moves from place to place (noun)

She was grateful for her friends' encouragement and reminders that the depression caused by the breakup was only transient and she would feel happier soon.

Few civilians understand the transient nature of the military and how often soldiers move from one post to the next.

He was skilled enough to get work wherever he went so he chose to be a transient in order to see the country.

transitory (TRAN-zih-tor-ee), adjective
Temporary and short-lived

The transitory stress of meeting her deadlines was worth the joy she found in her job on a day–to–day basis.

travesty (TRAV-ehs-tee), noun
An over-the-top, exaggerated, or twisted take on the truth of something; a distorted version

The sound of her singing was a travesty until after the surgery when her voice was returned to its former range.

trenchant (TREHN-chent), adjective
Forceful, meaningful, and emotionally heated

Their politics were different enough that they often engaged in trenchant debates but neither took them personally.

trifling (TRIY-fling), adjective
Unimportant; not worth dealing with; insignificant, referring to an amount or the importance of a thing

She saved the trifling paperwork for the end of the day so she could handle the major issues when she was most alert earlier in the day.

truculence (TRUK-yoo-lens), noun
The state of being eager and ready to fight over petty issues

The truculence that he had been known for throughout high school mellowed while he was in college to the point his friends from home barely recognized him.

truculent (TRUK-yoo-lehnt), adjective
Easily angered; having a chip on one's shoulder; defiant and aggressive
The young woman spent a good deal of time in detention because of her truculent attitude in the classroom.

truncate (TRUNG-kayt), verb
To shorten by cutting off an end, used figuratively and literally
The dance was unexpectedly truncated when the fire alarm went off, triggering the sprinklers.

turbid (TUR-bid), adjective
Muddy and unclear; stirred up, can be used literally or figuratively
She knew she would never find the ring she had dropped in the turbid river.

turgid (TER-jid), adjective
Swollen due to fluid; or excessively fancy and flowery, used to describe a way of speaking or writing; pompous
The turgid fruit practically exploded when the children bit into the flesh, dripping juices down their chins.
He meant his turgid speech to sound impressive but it only sounded as if he was putting on airs.

turmoil (TER-moyl), noun
A state of great confusion or agitation; frightening uncertainty
The country was thrown into turmoil after the assassination of the prime minister.

turpitude (TER-pih-tood) or (TER-pih-tyood), noun
Wicked, immoral behavior; evilness; obscene and vulgar actions
He lived a life of turpitude before cleaning up his act.

tutelage (TOOT-uh-lidj) or (TYOOT-uh-lidj), noun
Protection or guardianship; or the acts of a teacher or mentor; instruction
While the great works of art toured the country, they fell under the tutelage of the museums hosting them, so security was increased at each site.
She learned more about the business world in six weeks under her supervisor's tutelage than she had throughout her entire college career.

tyro (TIY-roh), noun
A beginner; someone new to a field of study or business
The firefighters respected each tyro more and more the longer they were willing to put up with the gentle hazing every new guy was put through.

ulterior (uhl-TEER-ree-ohr), adjective
Hidden; beyond what is acknowledged or admitted to
Since he didn't feel he deserved the promotion, the young man wondered if his boss had ulterior motives for giving it to him.

undulate (UN-jeh-layt) or (UN-dyeh-layt), verb
To move in a smooth, steady motion; to sway; to swing
The motion of the sea caused the ship to undulate in a soothing way, practically rocking the passengers to sleep.

untenable (uhn-TEN-ah-bul), adjective
Unjustifiable; impossible to defend or maintain an argument for
The entire group found his comments on a woman's role in workplace to be untenable and sexist.

untoward (un-TOHRD), adjective
Inappropriate; socially unacceptable and uncomfortable; improper
Everyone at the party tried to ignore his untoward behavior as the man got drunker and drunker.

unwarranted (un-WAR-rehn-ted), adjective
Having no justification or basis in fact
Enough of her friends were at the dance that she quickly decided her fears of being bored and alone all night had been unwarranted.

upbraid (up-BRAYD), verb
To scold; to criticize
The boys looked so miserable and their plans had failed so terribly that their mother couldn't bring herself to upbraid them for going against her wishes and trying to launch the raft into the river.

usurp (YOO-surp) or (YOO-zurp), verb
To take the place or power of another illegally
In the past, it was vital for a king to have a legitimate heir or else risk others trying to usurp the throne.

vagary (VAY-guh-ree), noun
An unexpected, unpredictable change; a sudden change that cannot be explained
Her mother was constantly amazed by the vagaries of teenage fashion and style.

vainglory (VAYN-glohr-ee), noun
Excessive and undeserved arrogance in oneself; extreme, undeserved arrogance
The young light designer's vainglory only made him look foolish in front of the older, more experienced stage hands.

valorous (VAH-ler-us), adjective
Marked by extreme bravery; daringly courageous
The valorous teen saved his little sisters from the fire after a candle tipped over in their room.

vapid (VA-pid), adjective
Uninteresting and unchallenging
His parents knew he was maturing when he brought home an intelligent and witty young woman instead of the vapid girls he usually dated.

variegated (VAYR-ih-gay-ted) or (VAYR-ee-gay-ted), adjective
Having different colored streaks or spots; marked by having variety, can be used literally or figuratively
The variegated leaves in early September were the first signs that autumn was coming and the leaves would soon be changing fully.

vehement (VEE-uh-ment), adjective
Intense; forceful; marked by strong feelings or emotions
The old woman was vehement in her insistence that her grandson go to college, even if she had to pay for it herself.

venal (VEE-nuhl), adjective

Corrupt; willing to take bribes; able to be paid off

The new warden fired every guard who had a venal reputation in order to restore order to the prison.

vendetta (ven-DEHD-dah), noun

A long, drawn out feud between two parties or families, usually implies a desire on at least one side to seriously damage the other side

Conservatives claim liberals have a vendetta against them while the liberals tend to claim just the opposite.

veneer (VIN-eer), noun

A false front or false face; a superficial and phony attitude

She emitted a veneer of happiness for the party but was actually very stressed over the deadline she faced at work the next day.

venerable (VEN-her-ah-bul), adjective

Due great respect, usually because of age, character, or wisdom

The venerable rabbi was sought for advice not only by his own synagogue but by other leaders in the community.

venial (VEE-nyul) or (VEE-nee-uhl), adjective

Slight and easy to forgive; minor, used to describe actions that aren't quite acceptable

The police took the girl home and made her tell her parents about her venial act of vandalism for spray painting the bridge rather than charge her with a crime because she had never done anything like it before.

veracious (ver-AY-shus), adjective

Consistently honest and truthful; accurate most of the time

The veracious newspaper frequently received praise on the national level for being unbiased and straightforward.

verbiage (VER-bee-idj) or (VER-bidj), noun

Speech or writing that is wordy; the use of too many words

The editor's job was to take the author's verbiage and make it easier for the average reader to understand clearly.

verbose (ver-BOHS), adjective
Using or having more words than necessary; using such flowery or technical language that the meaning is obscured
The professor was known to be so verbose that his students often had a hard time recognizing what was important and what could be ignored.

verdant (VER-duhnt), adjective
Lush and green, such as grass or other plants
The verdant park was the perfect and most romantic place he could think of to propose.

veritable (VEHR-ih-tuh-bul), adjective
Real or actual, often used to intensify a metaphor
He was so good at trivia games that they teased him that he was a veritable encyclopedia of trivial information.

vestige (VEST-idj), noun
A small amount; a trace; a tiny indication that something exists
The last vestiges of anxiety about owning her own home disappeared the first time she walked in the door after signing the paperwork.

vexation (VEKS-ay-shun), noun
Being annoyed or frustrated; or that which causes someone to be annoyed or frustrated
He tried to hide his vexation with the young woman who was holding up the line when he was already late for a meeting.
Although the vexations of high school seem important at the time, they become less so as time passes and people mature.

vicissitude (vis-SIHS-ah-tood) or (vis-SIHS-ah-tyood), noun
Regular and methodical changes and variations taking place over a very long time, usually pluralized; or unforeseen or unexpected changes, often leading one to another, usually pluralized
The two women, now old and gray, had known each other since childhood and had seen each other through all the vicissitudes of life.
Looking back at the diner where she had gotten her first job, the actress was amazed at the vicissitudes that had brought her to the awards podium.

V

vigilant (VIJ-eh-lent), adjective
Watchful; aware and attentive

The baby's aunt was even more vigilant than his parents because she was so nervous about something happening while she was babysitting.

vilify (VIL-ih-fiy), verb
To speak or write harshly and often incorrectly about something or someone; to insult cruelly

She took the high road and refused, in spite of embarrassing questions, to vilify her ex-husband in the press.

vindicate (VIN-dih-kayt), verb
To clear of charges or prove innocent; or to prove justified; to be proven right or correct

The testimony of the eye witness vindicated the wrongly accused man.

In spite of herself, the young mother felt vindicated when her husband had a hard time getting the baby bathed and dressed after he'd criticized her for how long it took.

Which Word?

Many words can be used as either a verb or an adjective. Vindicate (VIN-dih-kayt) is one of them. The verb to vindicate means to prove innocent. The adjective vindicate is the way someone feels when they have been proven innocent or their stance has been justified. When used as an adjective, the word is often vindicated. So it could be said that a wrongly accused man will feel vindicated once the evidence vindicates him.

virago (vuh-RAY-goh) or (vuh-RAH-goh), noun
An extraordinary woman of uncommon strength, courage, and vigor; or a woman considered noisy, violent, and demanding

Nearly every man who helped settle the American West had a virago by his side, willing to take every risk right along with him.

The president's secretary was such a virago that everyone from the customers to the president himself were just a little afraid of her.

virtu (vihr-TOO), noun

An appreciation for and love of art or the arts; or a grouping of fine art pieces taken or considered together

Few people expected a police officer to have such virtu that he quite happily spent his days off at the museum.

The virtu of boxes displayed at the museum were all that survived from the larger collection owned by the queen prior to the revolution.

virtuoso (vihr-choo-OH-soh) or (vihr-choo-OH-zoh), noun or adjective

A master in the field of study, usually the arts (noun) or showing mastery of the skills required for a specific field of study, usually the arts (adjective)

The university prided itself on hiring only virtuosos to teach even the most basic freshman classes.

The critics called the singer's virtuoso performance the best ever heard in the opera house.

visage (VIZ-idj), noun

The face; facial features or expressions; or the outward appearance

Regardless of the situation, he maintained a calm visage that didn't even hint at worry or concern.

The rocky visage of the cliff became more intimidating as the climbers got closer and could see it clearly.

viscous (VIHS-kuhs), adjective

Having a thick, gooey texture that does not flow easily

The students knew the lab experiment had gone wrong when the liquid, which was supposed to pour easily, turned into viscous ooze instead.

vitiate (VISH-ee-ayt), verb

To decrease the value; to make less worthy or worthwhile

The counselors were afraid the rules that were put in place to protect the program would actually vitiate it and hamper the children's success.

vituperate (vih-TOO-per-ayt) or (vih-TYOO-per-ayt), verb
To use harsh, blaming, and vicious language, especially against another person

> *The senator was known to vituperate against whichever group or organization had most recently spoken out against her pet projects, so no one paid her any attention.*

vituperative (vih-TOO-per-ah-tiv) or (vih-TYOO-per-ah-tiv), adjective
Abusive; unnecessarily harsh

> *She was shocked by the vituperative message her sister left on the answering machine after their recent quarrel.*

vivify (VIV-ih-fiy), verb
To make more interesting or lively; to make come alive

> *A good teacher can vivify even the dullest of subjects for a class.*

What I Meant to Say Was . . .

Don't get confused by words that look or sound almost identical. Vilify (VIL-ih-fiy) and vivify (VIV-ih-fiy) can easily be confused. To vilify is to spread lies and say nasty things about another person. To vivify is to energize or bring something to life. Just remember to read carefully!

---

vociferous (voh-SIHF-er-us), adjective
Loud and noisy; unrestrained and boisterous; generally referring to protests or cheers

> *The Red Sox were met with vociferous cheers and rowdy celebrations after winning the World Series for the first time in over eighty years.*

voluble (VOL-yuh-bul), adjective
Characterized by talking a great deal, usually implies speaking well and intelligently

> *The candidate's voluble style was effective because she could sound like an intellectual or a small-town girl, depending on which was appropriate.*

wary (WAHR-ee), adjective
Cautious; alert and on guard
A smart woman is wary but not afraid when she is out on her own after dark.

wean (WEEN), verb
To ease someone off of something they have become dependent on
The doctors noted it was time to wean him off the pain medication he'd been given after the surgery so he wouldn't become addicted.

whimsical (WHIM-sihk-uhl), adjective
Characterized by acting playfully or amusingly erratic; lighthearted; or dependent on chance; unpredictable
Although he had been dreading taking his sister and her friends to the fair, the children's whimsical enjoyment of the day turned out to be contagious and he enjoyed himself after all.

The weather in Scotland seemed whimsical throughout their vacation, bringing rain and fog one day and bright, warm sunshine the next.

witticism (WIT-ih-sihz-em), noun
A pun, joke, or funny remark
Her witticism was the perfect remedy for the tension that had been building in the staff meeting.

xenophobia (zeh-neh-FOH-bee-yah) or (zee-noh-FOH-bee-yah), noun
The irrational fear of anything or anyone from another country or foreign country
Although international travel tends to be an excellent cure for xenophobia, the people who suffer from it the most are usually the least likely to go overseas.

xerophyte (zihr-ih-FIYT), noun
Any plant that requires very little water in order to grow and thrive
Many gardeners will actually drown cacti not realizing they are xerophytes and therefore grow better without being watered on a weekly basis.

Y

xylography (ziy-LOG-raf-ee), noun
The act of making art or print using woodprints and blocks to transfer ink,
generally refers to a primitive technique
*Although it was eventually replaced by typesetting, originally, xylography
was considered a fast and efficient way to illustrate and print documents.*

xylophagous (ziy-LOF-ih-gus), adjective
Feeding on, living on, or burrowing into wood, as an insect
*Termites can cause nearly irreparable damage to wood structures because they
are xylophagous by nature.*

yare (YAR), adjective
Easily moved, steered or maneuverable, generally used when describing sailing vessels
*The small boat was yare in a way the captain of the large yacht wasn't expect-
ing, so he had to adjust his style to match the boat's responsiveness.*

yearling (YEER-ling), noun or adjective
A creature that is one year old (noun)
One year old (adjective)
*The yearlings in the petting zoo were popular attractions with the children
who were afraid of the older, larger animals.*
*The entire world watched the yearling government to see if the country would
settle into a democracy or if civil war would break out again.*

yen (YEN), noun
A longing; an urge or desire; craving
*The young man had always had a yen to travel to Ireland and see the town
where his grandfather had grown up.*

yeti (YEH-tee), noun
A large, hairy creature, rumored to live in the mountains
*The locals' stories about the yeti that roamed the mountainside were no longer
humorous now that the hikers were isolated and alone at their campsite.*

yew (YOO), noun
A particular type of evergreen tree, surrounded by myth and legend because of its extremely long life span

It was once believed that witches would gather under the boughs of the yew trees on the night of the full moon in order to cast spells and work magic.

zealot (ZEL-eht), noun
A person who believes so strongly in an idea, political party, or religion that it becomes more important than just about anything else

Even though there are zealots at either end of the political spectrum in the United States, most people consider something other than politics their top priority.

zeitgeist (ZIHT-giyst), noun
The defining spirit of a time; the overall mood of an era

The free-spirited zeitgeist of the 1920s was too quickly replaced by the despair of the Depression in the 1930s.

Z

Exercises

Exercise 1

Using the list of words in the back of the book, create a list of the words you think you already know the definitions of. Write them on a piece of paper. Double-check your definition against the one given in the book. If you get some of them wrong, study those carefully so you don't get your definition and the official one confused on a test.

Exercise 2

After completing Exercise 1, pick ten words you didn't know prior to getting this book. Use the definitions listed here as a guide to help you create your own, short definition for these words. Repeat this until you have defined all the new words. Put the lists aside and, several weeks from now, look at them again. If you can't remember the definition, study these words some more.

Exercise 3

Pick ten words randomly. Write a paragraph that uses those ten words in a way that actually makes sense and means something. Repeat the process until you have used all 1,000 words in a sentence at least once.

Exercise 4

Have some fun. Go through the list of words and create your own insults and compliments. Use at least two adjectives and a noun in each phrase. When you've got the hang of it, add a verb and write full sentences. Can you find ways to express yourself without the other person knowing what you're saying? Remember to be complimentary as well as insulting!

Exercise 5

You may have noticed that several words in the book can be used as different parts of speech. However, most words can be used as different parts of speech, not just the ones specifically mentioned. While every word in the book has been identified as one you may run across on the SAT or GRE tests, they may not appear in the exact form listed here. Pick a few words, perhaps ten or fifteen at a time, and try to figure out how they might change if they were used as an adverb or an adjective, past tense instead of present. Double-check your choices in the dictionary.

Exercise 6

For this exercise, you need to refer to the roots/prefixes guide in Appendix A. Examine the following list of twenty words. Some of the words are from this book; others aren't. Some are pretty difficult; some are pretty easy. Don't look up or confirm their definitions before you start this exercise. Next to each word, indicate whether each word has a positive, negative, or neutral connotation. After you have done that, use the roots/prefix guide to find the root in the word and make note of that. Don't worry about defining the word yet. For now, just come up with the correct roots. Now, double-check your work. How close did you come by breaking the word down using roots and prefixes? If you got every one of these correct, good for you. Take it up a notch by going to your dictionary and finding words you don't know at all. Break down those words the same way. (Hint: The answers to the twenty words given are on page 176 if you just can't figure them out! Just try first.)

- Revert
- Ultralight
- Circumference
- Remit
- Error
- Concession
- Misanthrope
- Ignorant
- Antagonist
- Hemorrhage
- Sacrosanct
- Corps
- Psychotropic
- Accelerate
- Divorce
- Entrust
- Supervision
- Automated
- Diverse
- Mobile

Exercise 7

Some of the sidebars in the text are about words that, without changing them in any way, could be more than one part of speech. This exercise takes that concept one step further. With many words, a small change in their spelling changes their part of speech without altering their meaning much. For example, reciprocity is a noun meaning a mutual exchange. Reciprocal, on the other hand, is an adjective meaning mutually exchanged. (You can look back at the defintions section of the book for fuller definitions of both words.) Now you can see how a small change in the spelling creates a small change in the meaning and a whole new part of speech. Following are twenty words from the text. These words can be used as other parts of speech by making slight changes. For each set of words, write a sentence using the first word. Then, write another sentence that maintains the meaning of your first sentence but uses the second word in the set, which is a different part of speech.

Example: The old miser stayed at home every evening, refusing even to rent a movie.

The old man's miserly ways kept him at home every evening without even a rented movie to watch.

1. penury   penurious
2. importune   importunate
3. complacency   complacent
4. abstinence   abstemious
5. ostracism   ostracize
6. sluggard   sluggish
7. verbiage   verbose
8. odium   odious
9. discretion   discreet
10. reciprocal   reciprocity

Answers for Exercise 6

- ■ Revert—neutral root: vert, vers (turn)
- ■ Ultralight—positive prefix: ultra (excessively)
- ■ Circumference—neutral prefix: circum (around)
- ■ Remit—neutral prefix: re (back, again)
- ■ Error—negative root: err (wander, mistake)
- ■ Concession—neutral root: ced, cede, cess (yield, go)
- ■ Misanthrope—neutral root: anthrop (man, mankind, humanity)
- ■ Ignorant—negative prefix: in, ig, il, im, ir (not)
- ■ Antagonist—negative prefix: anti (against, opposite)
- ■ Hemorrhage—neutral root: hem (blood)
- ■ Sacrosanct—positive root: sacr, sanct (holy)
- ■ Corps—neutral root: corp (body)
- ■ Psychotropic—neutral root: psych (mind)
- ■ Accelerate—neutral prefix: ad, ac, af, ag, an, ap, ar, as, at (to, forward)
- ■ Divorce—neutral prefix: di (two)
- ■ Entrust—neutral prefix: en, em (in, into)
- ■ Supervision—positive prefix: super (over, above)
- ■ Automated—neutral root: auto (self)
- ■ Diverse—neutral prefix: di (two)
- ■ Mobile—neutral root: mob, mot, mov (move)

Now go look up the words you don't know!

SAT Samples

The SAT writing section is made up of four parts: identifying errors in a sentence; improving or making sentences easier to understand; improving a paragraph; and a timed essay. The key to the first three sections is to maintain the meaning of the statement while making it grammatically correct. As you work on all the sections, keep in mind what you have learned in school, the hints from this book, and your own ear for words.

Hints for Finding Sentence Errors

First, remember the error must be in one of the marked sections of the sentence. Your best bet is to remember the grammar you've learned in school (or try to, anyway!) and look for common mistakes. If the error is glaring and you see it immediately, great! If you do not see it immediately, do not assume the sentence is correct. Here are two basic grammar reminders to help jog your memory.

Look at the pronouns. Are they the right form for their placement in the sentence? For example:

> *Candace took care of Nichelle and I while we were at the hotel.*
> A　　　　　　　　B　　　　　　　　　　C

The mistake is in section B; the sentence should read:

> *Candace took care of Nichelle and me while we were at the hotel.*

If you are unsure about the pronouns, break the sentence down. Get rid of everything extraneous: Candace took care of I. That's obviously incorrect. However, Candace took care of me is obviously correct. The form doesn't change simply because Nichelle is at the hotel as well.

Once you are certain the pronouns are correct, make sure the noun and the verb match. For example:

> *He is one of those people who need coffee or he can't wake up.*
> A　　　　　　　　　B　　　　　　　　C

Once again, the mistake is in section B. Do not be confused or thrown off by the plural word "people." While some people may need coffee, he is the one person being discussed. Therefore, he needs coffee. Notice we used the same trick of removing the excess in order to get to this answer. We broke it down to "He need coffee," which is obviously incorrect.

Hints for Improving Sentences

The same hints you used for finding sentence errors will serve you well when it comes time to improve sentences. Always start with the basics, then move on from there. Also, read the shortest option carefully. A well-written sentence is often concise, making it shorter. Do not choose the short sentence out of hand, however. It's a good idea to read it first, then read the other options.

Watch out for multiple conjunctions or strangely placed conjunctions. Sentences with several "ands" or with an "and" in an awkward place can be easily rewritten.

Simon wanted <u>three new video games for his birthday and a new watch and a digital camera.</u>

A. three new video games and a new watch and a digital camera for his birthday.

B. three new video games, a new watch, and a digital camera.

C. three new video games and a new watch and a digital camera.

D. three new video games, a new watch, and a digital camera for his birthday.

The correct answer is D. In option A, the "ands" make the sentence difficult to understand, even if the list of items is better organized. Options B and C change the meaning of the sentence by removing the phrase "for his birthday" (and C repeats the same mistake as A, as well). Option D is the choice that gives the list some organization, removes the unnecessary conjunctions, and maintains the meaning of the original sentence.

Do the parts of a series match? Are they the same tense or form? If not, change these things to improve the sentence.

Lionel and Daisy are happy dogs, <u>basking in the sun, playing together, and they chase their tails.</u>

A. basking in the sun, playing together, chase their tails.

B. basking in the sun, playing together, and chasing their tails.

C. bask in the sun, play together, and chase their tails.

D. ; basking in the sun, playing together, and chasing their tails.

The correct answer is B. Although too many conjunctions can confuse a sentence, simply removing them, as in option A, doesn't solve anything if the forms are not correct. In option C, even though the form of the actions match, their form does not follow the form of the rest of the sentence therefore this cannot be the correct choice. D adds a semicolon where one does not belong because the words following it do not make a complete sentence. Option B, on the other hand, corrects the form of all the actions and matches that form to the beginning of the sentence, making it the correct answer.

Check to see if the sentence is a run-on sentence or contains a comma splice. A comma splice can be remedied in so many different ways that for this example we will change the format and show you multiple ways to improve the sentence. Luckily, you will only be offered one correct option on the actual test.

We were late to the movie, Shelly was so late getting to the bus stop.

Those are actually two separate sentences instead of just one, so more than just a comma is required. Any of the following sentences are acceptable improvements:

A. We were late to the movie because Shelly was so late getting to the bus stop.

B. Shelly was so late getting to the bus stop that we were late getting to the movie.

C. We were late to the movie; Shelly had been late getting to the bus stop.

D. Since Shelly was so late getting to the bus stop, we were late getting to the movie.

Remember, in this particular case, all four of those options are correct ways to improve the sentence.

Hints for Improving Paragraphs

In this section of the test, you will be given a paragraph that needs to be rewritten in order to make it clearer, more concise, or grammatically correct. The format will be similar to the example here. Do not get nervous or worked up at the thought of improving an entire paragraph. Take it section by section. Remember, it's a multiple choice section so take it one question at a time and keep breathing.

(1) Because William Shakespeare is best known for his plays, that he wrote sonnets too is often forgotten. (2) This is a shame because his poetry is beautiful. (3) It is thought-provoking. (4) It deserves the same praise as his plays. (5) His plays are unquestionably brilliant but still they are not all he was capable of writing. (6) More people should know of his sonnets and have read them. (7) They will appreciate them and Shakespeare more.

1. Sentence 1, reproduced below, can best be rewritten in which way?

Because William Shakespeare is best known for his plays, that he wrote sonnets too is often forgotten.

A. Because William Shakespeare is best known for his plays; that he wrote sonnets too is often forgotten.
B. Since William Shakespeare is best known for his plays, the fact that he wrote sonnets is too often forgotten.
C. Since William Shakespeare is best known for his plays, the fact that he wrote sonnets as well is often forgotten.
D. William Shakespeare is best known for his plays, and it is often forgotten that he wrote sonnets, too.

Option C is the correct answer. Option A adds a semicolon where no semicolon belongs. Again, as in the previous section, the words before and after the semicolon do not form complete sentences. Many students do not understand semicolons well and therefore get impressed into thinking that if an option contains a semicolon, it must be correct. Don't fall into this trap. Option B is tricky. It is a correct sentence, but it changes the meaning of the original, albeit slightly. In the original sentence, "too" means "also." In option B, "too" modifies "often." In other words, Shakespeare's sonnets are not only forgotten often, they are forgotten too often. And that's not what the original sentence is saying. Option D offers a correct sentence, just not a very well-written one. This choice doesn't improve the paragraph much. Simply replacing one poorly written sentence with another is not the goal. Option C, the correct option, is clear and concise, and maintains the meaning of the original sentence.

2. How can sentences 2, 3, and 4, reproduced below, best be rephrased?

This is a shame because his poetry is beautiful. It is thought-provoking. It deserves the same praise as his plays.

A. This is a shame because his poetry is brilliant, thought provoking, and deserving of praise.
B. This shame is because his poetry is brilliant, thought provoking, and deserving of praise.
C. His poetry is brilliant, thought provoking, and deserving of praise so it is a shame that people forget he wrote it.
D. This is a shame because his poetry is brilliant and thought provoking and deserving of praise.

Option A is the correct answer. Option B changes the meaning of the sentence. There is no shame in one's poetry being brilliant, and yet that is what this sentence claims. Watch out for different meanings using similar words. Options C and D are, technically, correct sentences but they are awkward. Therefore, they cannot be the best way to improve a paragraph. Option A is grammatically correct and, quite frankly, pleasing to the ear. Remember to use your own knowledge of language and words as well as your understanding of grammar.

3. Sentence 5, reproduced below, can best be rewritten in which way?

His plays are unquestionably brilliant but still they are not all he was capable of writing.

A. He was not only capable of writing unquestionably brilliant plays. He was also capable of writing poetry.

B. While his plays are unquestionably brilliant, they are not all he was capable of writing.

C. His plays are unquestionably brilliant but he was capable of writing others.

D. While his plays are unquestionably brilliant, they are not the only writing he was capable of.

Option B is the correct answer. Option A is correct but hardly improves the paragraph. It creates two simple sentences where one slightly more complex sentence does a better job expressing the feelings of the author. Option C, again, changes the meaning of the sentence. The word "others," in this case, means other plays. Arguably, other less brilliant, more mediocre plays. While Shakespeare was probably capable of writing mediocre plays, they are hardly the subject of this paragraph. Option D ends a sentence in a preposition, which, as you know, is unacceptable in formal writing. Option B gets the point of the sentence across in a clear, concise manner.

4. How can sentences 6 and 7, reproduced below, be rewritten more effectively?

More people should know of his sonnets and have read them. They will appreciate them and Shakespeare more.

A. More people should read Shakespeare's sonnets to appreciate both of them more.

B. People who read Shakespeare's sonnets will appreciate them if they were read more.

C. More people should read Shakespeare's sonnets. People who do so will appreciate his poetry and Shakespeare himself even more.

D. People should know about Shakespeare's poetry. They will appreciate his sonnets more and Shakespeare, too.

Option C is the correct answer. Option A makes it sound as if Shakespeare wrote only two sonnets. Option B is an awkward sentence that does not address appreciating Shakespeare more, it mentions only his sonnets. Option D is correct but immature and adds the unnecessary "and" clause at the end. Option C combines knowing and reading Shakespeare's poetry, as it is hard to read them without knowing of them, and cleans up the sentences nicely.

Hints for the Timed Essay

The final verbal section of the SAT is a timed essay. You will be given the subject of the essay at the time of the test but not before. This makes it difficult but not impossible to prepare for this section of the test. The best aid you can give yourself is to write essays. Write on any topic you choose—and don't always choose topics you have a broad knowledge of already. It won't do you any good to have written practice essays on your favorite sport or political cause if you know them so well that you can write them without having to think critically about them. Be aware that the SAT testers love to give quotes and ask your opinion on the quote. Now that you know this, writing an essay on an unfamiliar quote may be a good place to start (hint, hint).

The essay is timed, and you have twenty-five minutes to write it. Learn how much you can write in twenty-five minutes. Set the kitchen timer and write until it goes off. This will help you discover how much time you want to put toward the introduction, the body, and the summation of the essay. Being able to write a strong essay while sitting at your kitchen table or in the library increases your chances of being able to write a strong essay under the pressure in the real test-taking conditions.

Be careful not to use too flowery language. Yes, it might be tempting to show off all the new words you have learned. And yes, the testers do want to see that you have a grasp of the language and a relatively large vocabulary. However, you still need to be careful. Consider adjectives and adverbs to be the seasonings you add to a stew (your essay). Used in the right amount, they will enhance the flavor and enjoyment of your essay. Used in the wrong amounts—too often or even incorrectly—they simply distract from the flavor and overall effect of the writing. Also, no word is impressive if it is used incorrectly. Unless you are certain the word is appropriate, don't use it.

The most important thing to remember during the SAT is to stay as calm and as relaxed as possible. If you are reading this book, you've obviously put some time and effort into studying and preparing yourself. Trust the knowledge you have gained and don't panic!

Ready for some sample test questions? Good. The answers are at the end. Good luck.

Finding Errors in Sentences

Choose the underlined section in which there is a mistake.

1. The woman, who's car was covered in snow, was an hour late to work
        A   B   C
   due to the storm.
       D

   __ A
   __ B
   __ C
   __ D

2. After the run-down building was razed, the lot had become a play-
        A   B   C
   ground for the neighborhood children
                    D

   __ A
   __ B
   __ C
   __ D

3. When the flood waters, who had threatened to breach the levee,
      A   B   C
   receded, everyone in town celebrated.
                D

   __ A
   __ B
   __ C
   __ D

4. Sam didn't understand why Sally stayed home when she could of
      A   B   C
gone out with him.
     D

_ A

_ B

_ C

_ D

5. The meteorologists were predicting the worst storm in a century but
                A   B
it swerved at the last moment and didn't hardly brush the coast.
   C   D

_ A

_ B

_ C

_ D

Improving Sentences

Choose the option that best improves the underlined section of each sentence.

1. Since she was on a diet, she ordered only salad and tea with no dressing.

    A. salad and tea and no dressing.

    B. no dressing with her salad and tea.

    C. salad, tea, no dressing.

    D. salad, with no dressing, and tea.

    E. Sentence is correct.

2. When the movie was sold out, they went dancing instead.

    A. When the movie was sold out; they went

    B. Since the movie was sold out, they went

    C. Due to the fact that they went dancing the movie was sold out

    D. Since the movie was sold out; they went

    E. Sentence is correct.

3. The children were <u>so exhausted and they fell asleep immediately</u>.

    A. so exhausted that they fell asleep immediately.

    B. so exhausted so they fell asleep immediately.

    C. so exhausted which they fell asleep immediately.

    D. so exhausted and so they fell asleep immediately.

    E. Sentence is correct.

4. The pitcher had <u>injured his arm, which made his aim erratic</u>.

    A. injured his arm so that his aim was erratic.

    B. injured his arm that made his aim erratic.

    C. injured his arm so that his aim was erratically.

    D. injured his arm, made his aim erratic.

    E. Sentence is correct.

5. Her room was <u>such a mess, she could never find anything</u>.

    A. such a mess so that she could never find anything.

    B. such a mess that she could never find anything.

    C. such a mess and because of it she could never find anything.

    D. such a mess because she could never find anything.

    E. Sentence is correct.

Improving Paragraphs

Choose the option that best improves the following paragraph.

(1) If you choose to adopt a dog from a rescue organization, it is a generous and loving thing to do. (2) Many dogs are given up for reasons that do not make them bad pets. (3) Their owners just can't keep them any longer. (4) Often, rescue animals make better pets because they are so grateful at being adopted. (5) You also know what you're getting in terms of the animal's background like if it was abused. (6) These are two of the many reasons to adopt a rescue dog. (7) So if you want a good, loving pet considering going through rescue. (8) Plus you do a good thing.

1. How can sentence 1, reproduced below, best be rewritten?

If you choose to adopt a dog from a rescue organization, it is a generous and loving thing to do.

    A. You are being generous and loving when you adopt a dog from a rescue organization.

    B. Choosing to adopt a dog from a rescue organization is a generous and loving step to take.

    C. To choose to adopt a pet from rescue is a choice that is generous and loving.

    D. It is a generous and loving choice to choose to adopt a pet from rescue.

2. How can sentences 2 and 3, reproduced below, best be combined/rewritten?

Many dogs are given up for reasons that do not make them bad pets. Their owners just can't keep them any longer.

    A. Many of the dogs given up to rescue are not bad pets. Their owners just cannot keep them any longer.

    B. For many reasons, they are bad pets and their owners cannot keep them any longer.

    C. Their owners cannot keep them any longer; which doesn't make them bad pets.

    D. They are not bad pets so that's not why their owners cannot keep them any longer.

3. How can sentences 4, 5, and 6, reproduced below, best be combined?

Often, rescue animals make better pets because they are so grateful at being adopted. You also know what you're getting in terms of the animal's background like if it was abused. These are two of the many reasons to adopt a rescue dog.

    A. Only two of the reasons to adopt a rescue pet is they are grateful and you know if they've been abused.

B. There are many reasons to adopt rescue pets. Including them being grateful and you knowing about abuse.

C. If the rescue pet was abused, you will know about it and be grateful. So will the pet.

D. While there are many reasons to adopt a rescue pet. one reason is you will know about the dog's background and if there was any previous abuse. Another reason is rescue pets are very loving and grateful for being adopted.

4. How can sentences 7 and 8, reproduced below, best be combined?

So if you want a good, loving pet considering going through rescue. Plus you do a good thing.

A. Consider going through rescue to adopt a dog to get a loving dog and do a good thing.

B. Consider adopting a dog through rescue. You will get a good, loving pet and do a good thing.

C. It is a good thing to consider adopting a good, loving dog. Especially through rescue.

D. It is a good thing to consider, especially through rescue, adopting a good loving dog.

Answer Key		
Finding Errors in Sentences	**Improving Sentences**	**Improving Paragraphs**
1. A	1. D	1. B
2. C	2. B	2. A
3. B	3. A	3. D
4. C	4. E	4. B
5. D	5. B	

GRE Samples

This book addresses three parts of the verbal section of the GRE: sentence completion, analogies, and antonyms. The verbal section of the test itself also includes essays. However, this book will be most helpful to you in the other sections, so that is where we will focus our attention.

Sentence Completion

Hints for Examples with One Blank

Look for particular words. Certain words will give you a hint as to which word will complete the sentence best. "And/but" or "therefore/however" or words like them are potential clues in any sentence.

If a sentence uses "and" or "therefore," whatever comes after that will follow in the same general theme. So, if your sentence reads: *Ann was always the life of the party,* **therefore** *everyone was always* _____ *to see her arrive*, then you should look for a word that continues the theme of Ann being a great person to have at a party. The positive of Ann's attitude is balanced by the positive of Ann's presence. The general theme of the sentence has stayed the same. The word elated would complete this sentence well. The "life of the party" is a positive statement as is "elated." Therefore, the general theme of the sentence has been maintained—as you knew it would be because of the word "therefore."

The words "but" or "however" will signify the opposite. At some point, the overall theme in the sentence is going to change. So, if the sentence reads: *Ann was usually* _____ , *but people invited her to parties anyway because they felt sorry for her*, then you should look for a word that suggests people invite Ann out of pity rather than enjoyment. The negative of Ann's presence is countered by the positive of inviting her to the party anyway. The general theme of the sentence changed. The word *morose* would complete this sentence well. "Morose" has a negative connotation while being invited to parties has a positive one. Thus, as we have established, the general theme of the sentence changed—as you expected it to when you first read the word "but."

Find the hint. Every sentence will have a hint phrase or phrases. Find that, and completing the sentence becomes that much easier.

The sentence *The day was* _____ is simply too vague. There is no way to know if you are providing the best answer or not. Luckily for you, you will not find vague sentences like that on the GRE.

The sentence *Considering it was February in New England, the day was surprisingly* _____ on the other hand can be completed. The hint has told you three things. First, it is February, a cold time of the year no matter where you are in the United States. Second, it involves New England, a notoriously cold part of the country. Third, the weather is surprising. You now know you are looking for weather that would be unexpected during a New England February.

The additional information in the sentence isn't there just to confound and confuse you. Some of it is there to guide you. Read every word carefully and find your hints.

Pick the right word. There are two schools of thought on how to pick the right word to complete a sentence. The one you choose is going to come down to personal preference and learning style. Both will work, so choose the method that is fastest *and* most effective for you. This is a timed test!

The first method is to write your own sentence. This involves ignoring the answers completely until you have figured out the sentence well enough to fill in the blank on your own. Do not waste time trying to come up with a GRE word. Fill in the blank with the easiest, simplest word you can find that makes sense. Once you have a word that makes sense then look at the answers to find a synonym for the word you have come up with yourself. Consider this option if you can think calmly and clearly during tests and believe you won't freeze up. If, however, you question your ability to come up with a word on your own, even a simple word, under the stress of test-taking conditions, you might want to consider the next option.

The second option is to read the sentence and then put each answer into the blank. Eliminate any word that simply makes no sense. Reserve any words that might work or words whose definitions you do not know. Once you have eliminated the words you can, work with what you have left. If you have only one word left, that's obviously the correct answer. If you have more than one word and you know their definitions, try to pick the *best* answer. If you are left with a word whose meaning you do not know and one whose definition you are certain you know, and the word you know works, choose it.

Hints for Examples with Two Blanks

Use the hints you used for the examples with one blank. They will still work. Two blanks aren't necessarily more difficult, and the same rules still apply.

Solve for one blank at a time. Remember, since both words in the answer set must work for that answer to be the best one, if you find an answer set in which the first word simply does not fit in the first blank, eliminate it. No matter how perfect the second word may be for the second blank, this answer will not be the best one.

Fill in the blanks with simple words. This will allow you make sure you know what the sentence is trying to say. Once you find simple words that make the sentence meaningful, it will be easier to find the best answer out of all of the answers given.

Look for relationships between the words in the blanks. For example, if you are given the sentence *The coffee was _____ and _____, so it woke her right up*, you can easily find the relationship—and the hint. (Reread the tips on completing sentences with one blank if you've forgotten about the hint!) The relationship between the words is indicated by the fact that both of the words will describe the coffee. The hint is, of course, the phrase "so it woke her right up." Both words are going to have something to do with waking her—the effect of the relationship. Finally, you can also look for the word "and." This indicates that the relationship is consistent, that the theme of the sentence stays the same. See how all the hints can be used together to help solve for two blanks? Simple words that could complete this sentence might be fresh/hot or strong/black.

The same hints apply to the sentence *The coffee was _____ but _____, so she drank it only for the caffeine, not for enjoyment.* Let's break it down again. Once again, the relationship between the words is that they both describe the coffee. The hint is the phrase "so she drank it only for the caffeine, not for enjoyment." This indicates that at least one of the words is going to describe something less than enjoyable. Finally, the word "but" shows a change in theme within the sentence. This should make you think that the first word is more positive while the second word is the one that is less enjoyable. Simple words that could complete this sentence might be strong/cold or even available/burned.

Analogies

Use the process of elimination. The words in the answers must have a relationship. Therefore, you can eliminate any answer sets that contain words with no relationship.

The words in the answers must have a similar relationship to the relationship of the words given in the example. Therefore, if the words in the example have a cause-and-effect relationship, you can eliminate any answer where the words given do not have a cause-and-effect relationship.

Write your own very simple sentence using the words in the example.

For *cold : shiver*, you could write, "The cold makes you shiver." Now you know you are looking for something that causes something else. Eliminate any options that do not have a causal relationship.

For *elate : please*, you could write, "To elate means to please." You now know you are looking for synonyms. Eliminate any options that do not have similar definitions.

Work backward if necessary.

With the example, *torso : head*, it may be easier to write the simple sentence: "A head is on top of a torso." You are looking for an option with a similar relationship.

REMEMBER! If you work backward from the example, you must work backward in the options! The testers could easily give *computer : desk* as a trick answer. If, in your haste, you have forgotten that you are working backward from the example, that answer could seem reasonable. After all, a computer is on top of a desk. However, since you must reverse the answers as well, choosing this response would really be saying that a desk is on top of a computer. Don't let the pressure of a timed test cause you to make such an easily avoidable mistake.

Always—always—read all of the options. The GRE asks for *the best answer.* You may find two answers that could work. One will be close. The other will be closer. If you stop at the first close one, you will miss the right one.

Don't eliminate a word out of hand simply because you don't know it. Go through the answers that contain words you can define. Eliminate as many of those as possible before deciding if the option you are unsure about can be eliminated—or not. It may be the right one.

Don't panic if you don't know one of the words in the example. Consider what you *do* know. You probably know the other word in the example. You know it has to have some kind of a relationship to the other word. You probably know most of the words in the answers.

Look to the answers. Do any of the answers *not* have relationships? Eliminate those immediately. Study the relationships there. Do any of the words in the answer ring any kind of bells with the word you know in the example?

You cannot skip any questions so an educated guess is better than a blind one. Focus on what you *do* know and eliminate from there.

Antonyms

If you know the example word, great! Remember, the antonym must have a relationship to the example. Eliminate any words that have no connection whatsoever to the example. Then, eliminate the synonyms. You're left with the antonym. And you're done!

If you don't know the example word *at all*, don't panic. Look at the answers. Do you know any of them? Odds are you will know some of them. Eliminate any answers you *know* do not have a relationship with the example word. These might be words you are comfortable enough with to know most of their antonyms, or they could be words that are completely different parts of speech from the example. An adjective cannot be an antonym for a verb.

Are any of the answers stronger, more extreme words than others? GRE testers tend to tilt the answers to one extreme or another. Eliminate any word that has a tepid or bland definition. For example, *egocentric* is a much stronger word than *arrogant*. If you are at a loss, consider reserving *egocentric* but consider eliminating *arrogant*.

Again, these hints will hopefully narrow it down for you and an educated guess, as we've stated, is better than a blind one.

If you think you know the word but aren't completely sure, that's okay, too. What kind of word is the example? Does it have a positive or negative connotation? What does it imply?

What kinds of words are the answers? Eliminate any option that has the same connotation or implies the same feeling. Remember, you are looking for differences, not similarities.

Finally, remember to eliminate any answer that has no opposite. Some nouns, for instance, have no opposite. There is nothing opposite of chair. Or, more subtly, there is nothing opposite of prejudice. If an answer cannot have an opposite, it cannot have, or in this case *be*, an antonym. Eliminate it out of hand.

Essays

A quick word about the essays: Obviously, the essays for the GRE are more complex than the essays for the SATs. More will, and should, be expected of you. However, if you start with the same basic rules outlined in the SAT Samples section, you will be one step ahead. Those are good rules to follow anytime you are writing. Whether you're writing a test essay, a report for the board of directors, or a letter to your grandmother, it's best to build on the basics. In brief, remember to limit your use of flowery and ornate language. You do not want to smother the meaning of the essay in adjectives and adverbs, especially the analytical section. Also, remember that it is better to leave out a word than to use one incorrectly. For a greater explanation of these tips, flip back to the SAT Samples section. Your foundation was built on the SATs, too, and a strong foundation is vital if you want to build anything worthwhile.

Now, if you think you're ready, here are some sample questions. The answers are at the end. Good luck!

Completing Sentences (One Blank)

1. As a/n _____ , she appreciated fine wines and a proper presentation.
   A. miser
   B. dilettante
   C. ascetic
   D. connoisseur

2. The _____ still made people smile and weep melancholy tears years after the old king's death.
   A. elegy
   B. eulogy
   C. console
   D. platitude

3. Even though she was financially secure, the memory of her
_____ past made it difficult for her to spend money frivo-
lously.
   A. preternatural
   B. impecunious
   C. miserly
   D. sedentary

4. The _____ attacks against his opponent ended up hurting,
rather than helping, his own party.
   A. conspicuous
   B. licentious
   C. punctilious
   D. vituperative

5. The old woman was convinced that every bad day was _____
by a sleepless night.
   A. distended
   B. inveigled
   C. presaged
   D. renounced

Completing Sentences (Two Blanks)

1. Great comics can often _____ against current political events
while _____ them at the same time.
   A. insinuate/lamenting
   B. inveigle/lampooning
   C. imbue/lauding
   D. impair/lingering

2. Over the years, her reasonable sense of _____ morphed into
a/n _____ reluctance to spend money on anything.
   A. discountenance/untoward
   B. frugality/miserly
   C. kith/stoic
   D. mettle/aberrant

3. Although the price was _____ coming from the West Coast, the young couple thought it was money well spent when they looked over the _____ that is Niagara Falls.
    A. exorbitant/cataract
    B. glacial/risible
    C. voluble/palate
    D. inconsequential/nadir

4. The _____ of the 1970s was a combination of _____ disregard for societal norms and radical activism.
    A. paean/nefarious
    B. odium/hirsute
    C. zeitgeist/blithe
    D. conviction/quiescent

5. The arrival of the police at the club turned the _____ customer into a _____ coward in the blink of an eye.
    A. tractable/whimsical
    B. obstreperous/pusillanimous
    C. nominal/quiescent
    D. jocular/contumacious

Analogies

1. lament : elegy
    A. yeti : omen
    B. prudence : eccentricity
    C. edible : comestible
    D. invalid : zealot

2. orator : orate
    A. whimsical : witticism
    B. braggart : preen
    C. fallacy : reverence
    D. robust : rotund

3. Obdurate : malleable
   A. glib : ornate
   B. truculent : punctilious
   C. impregnable : untenable
   D. ineffable : banal

4. Elusive : explicit
   A. vituperate : acclaim
   B. impromptu : improvident
   C. panacea : nostrum
   D. panegyric : accolade

5. Multifarious : heterogeneous
   A. remorse : elation
   B. palpable : frivolous
   C. renege : undulate
   D. trifling : nugatory

Antonyms

1. obfuscate
   A. occlude
   B. divulge
   C. imbue
   D. truncate

2. accede
   A. kowtow
   B. vivify
   C. renounce
   D. quaff

3. pacifist
   A. mercenary
   B. zealot
   C. opportunist
   D. denizen

4. raze
   A. yare
   B. obtrude
   C. bolster
   D. deign

5. fugacious
   A. deleterious
   B. servile
   C. aesthetic
   D. perennial

Answer Key			
Completing Sentences (One Blank)	Completing Sentences (Two Blanks)	Analogies	Antonyms
1. D	1. B	1. C	1. B
2. A	2. B	2. B	2. B
3. B	3. A	3. D	3. A
4. D	4. C	4. A	4. C
5. C	5. B	5. D	5. D

Appendix A

Roots, Prefixes, and Suffixes, or How to Figure Out What a Word Means When You're Really Stumped

Often you will come across a word you just don't know. The best thing to do at that point is to find a dictionary and look it up. However, that is not always an option—such as in the middle of a standardized test! So what do you do then? Knowing the roots of words can be helpful at times like this. If you can understand the root and combine it with its context in the sentence, it will be easier to figure out the general meaning of the word even if you still don't know the exact definition. It's a good trick to have up your sleeve when you can't get to a dictionary.

Just to review, a *root* is a most basic element of a word that has meaning—it's the basis from which the word is derived. Roots can be positive, negative, or neutral. The meaning of the root affects the word in which it is used. Therefore, generally speaking, if a root has a positive implication, the word itself will have a positive implication, such as *vital*. A negative root tends to indicate a negative word, such as *malicious*. A neutral root may indicate a neutral word, such as *manuscript*, or it may be part of a positive or negative word, such as *empower* or *adverse*. All of the suffixes listed here are neutral, but some roots and prefixes intensify or amplify the word. In these examples, intensifying roots and prefixes are listed with the positive roots and prefixes. Obviously there are exceptions to these rules (aren't there always?) but they are a good place to start. Don't worry if you can't find the roots in the words in the previous examples; they are described in greater detail in the lists that follow. Prefixes and suffixes attach to the beginning and end of words, respectively, to change their meaning in some way.

Following this is a very basic list of roots, prefixes, and suffixes. There are hundreds more, but these will help give you a starting point. Even though a simplistic definition is given next to each word, if you do not know the word, look it up either here or in a dictionary. Several of the words given as examples are not in this book. Some of them you will know; others you will not. You might want to keep a dictionary next to you while you read this appendix. After all, you're not sitting in a test right now, right?

Roots

Positive/Intensifying Roots
Am, amic (love, friend): as in amenable (friendly and open to an idea)
Fid (faith, trust): as in fidelity (faithfulness)
Magn (great): as in magnificent (awe-inspiring; better than the rest)
Sacr, sanct (holy): as in sacred (holy) and sanctimonious (holier than thou)
Soph (wise): as in sophisticated (worldly, wise)
Ver (true): as in aver (to state as true)
Vit, viv (life, lively): as in vital (required for life) or vivify (to enliven)

Negative Roots
Err (wander, mistake): as in aberrant (wandered from the norm)
Fall, fals (untrue, false): as in fallacious (not true)
Fug (flee): as in refugee (one who flees his home)
Mal (bad): as in malicious (to wish someone harm)
Mor, mort (death, die): as in mortify (to embarrass to the point of wishing for death)
Vinc, vict, vanq (to conquer): as in victorious (to win or succeed against the odds)

Neutral Roots
Agri (field, land, farm): as in agriculture (of the land)
Annu, enni (year): as in perennial (returning yearly)
Anthrop (man, mankind, humanity): as in anthropologist (one who studies the history and cultures of humanity)

Aqua (water): as in aquarium (a container of water used to keep fish as pets)

Auto (self): as in autonomous (being self-sufficient)

Brev (short, brief): as in abbreviate (to shorten)

Cap, capt, cepte, cip (take): as in capture (to steal or trap)

Carn (flesh): as in carnivore (one who eats meat)

Ced, cede, cess (yield, go): as in accede (to yield to a demand)

Chrono (time): as in anachronistic (out of time and place)

Cit, citat (call, start): as in citation (a summons or call to court)

Corp (body): as in corporeal (of the body)

Domin (rule): as in dominion (the area one rules or to control an area)

Gen (kind, birth, origin, race): as in gender (sex at birth) or general (of the usual kind)

Hem (blood): as in hematite (a blood red mineral)

Jac, jact, jec (throw): as in eject (to throw out)

Loqu, locut (talk): as in elocution (the art of speaking well)

Mob, mot, mov (move): as in motorized (moving due to an engine) or motion (movement)

Nat (born): as in natural (unchanged from its creation)

Ora (speak, pray): as in orate (to give a public speech)

Pater, part (father): as in patriarchal (governed or ruled by men)

Phon (sound): as in phonetics (the study of how words sound)

Psych (mind): as in psychological (of or in the mind)

Sed, sess (sit): as in sedate (calm)

Sci (know): as in prescience (knowing something before it happens)

Script (write): as in manuscript (written document)

Spec, spect (look at): as in spectacle (something worth watching)

Tors, tort (twist): as in contort (to twist into unnatural shapes)

Urb (city): as in suburban (outside of the city)

Vert, vers (turn): as in invert (to turn in a different direction) or adverse (turned away from a positive path)

Prefixes

Positive/Intensifying Prefixes

Arch (chief): as in archenemy (worst enemy or greatest adversary)

Bene (good, well): as in benefit (an extra good or a bonus that comes along with something else) or beneficial (good for you)

Extra (beyond, outside): as in extrapolate (to see beyond what is given or stated)

Hyper (above, excessively): as in hyperactive (overly active)

Pro (for, before, in front of): as in professor (one who teaches in front of a class)

Super (over, above): as in superlative (better than all the others)

Ultra (excessively): as in ultramodern (using materials and ideas only recently available)

Negative Prefixes

Anti (against, opposite): as in antithesis (the direct opposite)

Contra (against): as in contravene (to work against)

De (down, away from): as in descry (to put down)

Dis, di, dif (not, apart): as in different (not the same)

Ex, e, ef (out, off, from): as in egress (to go out or away from) or effigy (an image made from another)

In, ig, il, im, ir (not): as in ignoble (not noble) or irresponsible (not responsible)

Mal, male (bad, badly): as in maleficent (harmful or evil)

Mis (wrong, ill, not): as in misdeed (a mistake or poor action)

Non (not): as in nonentity (a person who does not exist)

Ob, oc, of, op (against): as in obstreperous (intentionally difficult) or obfuscate (to work against in order to confuse or make unclear)

Sub, suc, suf, sug (under): as in submerge (to go under water)

Un (not): as in unworthy (not worthy)

Under (below): as in underling (one who is of lower rank or importance)

Neutral Prefixes

Ab, abs (from, away from): as in abstain (to stay away from)

Ad, ac, af, ag, an, ap, ar, as, at (to, forward): as in attend (go to)

Ambi (both): as in ambidextrous (to use both hands equally)

Ante (before): as in antecedent (going before)

Auto (self): as in automatic (happening by itself without thought or decision)

Bi (two): as in bicameral (having two parts or chambers)

Cata (down): as in catatonic (unresponsive)

Circum (around): as in circumvent (to bypass or go around)

Com, co, con (with, together): as in conjoin (to bring together)

Di (two): as in divide (to split into two or more pieces)

En, em (in, into): as in empower (literally, to put power into)

In, il, im, ir (in, into): as in insert (to add in) or impale (to pierce or stab into)

Inter (between, among): as in intertwine (to wind through and among)

Intra, intro (within): as in introspection (looking within oneself)

Meta (change): as in metabolize (to chemically change within the body)

Mono (one): as in monologue (a speech in a play given by one person)

Multi (many): as in multicultural (made up of people from many different cultures)

Neo (new): as in neologism (a new word or phrase)

Pan (all, every): as in pandemic (widespread; throughout all areas)

Per (through): as in peruse (to read completely through)

Peri (around, near): as in periscope (a viewfinder that allows submarines to see all around the surface of the ocean)

Pre (before): as in precedent (something that comes before)

Re (back, again): as in rebate (to give back money)

Se (apart): as in separate (to keep or put apart)

Syl, sym, syn, sys (with, together): as in synonymous (meaning the same)

Trans (across, beyond, through): as in transport (to move from one place to another)

Suffixes

Ac, ic (like, pertaining to): as in acidic (like acid)

Cy (state of being): as in redundancy (the state of being redundant or repetitive)

Eer, er, or (person who): as in minister (one who serves the people)

Ist (dealer, doer): as in opportunist (one who looks out for himself)

Ize, ise (make): as in criticize (to make critical remarks)

Tude (state of): as in aptitude (the state of being able)

Appendix B

Common Mistakes

Beware to All Who Enter Here

The English language is a complex one, and we, as a society, tend to be lazy when it comes to language. This is not necessarily a bad thing. This way of speaking gives our language color and flavor. However, laziness and collo-quialisms (look it up if you need to; it's in the main body of the text!) have no place in formal essays. If you are writing for the SAT or the GRE, the testers expect you to be able to write the way the language is supposed to be used, not the way it is used in everyday conversation.

This appendix addresses some of the more common mistakes made with both words and grammar. Perhaps these are not the mistakes you make. You should still be aware of them and let them be a guide to help you figure out what mistakes you might make.

Words

Already/All ready

It is easy to interchange these two because, after all, they are the same word, right? Only they aren't the same word and actually have very different meanings. *Already* means something has already occurred or been accomplished, as in *She had already studied for the test so she was able to go to the movies with her friends.* This is very different from *all ready*, which means *prepared*, as in *The room was all ready for the party*. You can always use a synonym if you can't remember but it's best to learn the different definitions so you can use these words, as well their synonyms, properly.

Appendix/Appendices

An appendix is a section at the back of the book that adds necessary information that just didn't fit in the main text. This is an appendix—the main purpose of the book is to teach vocabulary, so grammar tips weren't particularly appropriate for the main text. However, the vocabulary is geared to people studying for the SAT or the GRE. In light of that, it seemed appropriate to have grammar tips in here somewhere. Thus, they were added to the appendices. Notice that change? That change is the point of this piece of information. When there is one additional section at the end of a book, it is an *appendix (uh-PEN-diks)*. Currently, there is a debate over how to pluralize the word "appendix." Some dictionaries and sources state "appendices" *(uh-PEN-dih-seez)* is the only truly correct way to do so. Others state "appendixes" *(uh-PEN-diks-es)* is as correct as "appendices." However, as with the GRE, I recommend you deal with the *best* answer. "Appendices" has been recognized as correct for longer, therefore your safest, smartest bet is to use "appendices." Remember, one appendix, several appendices.

Between/Among

These two words are often confused. They seem interchangeable. However, they are not. *Between* is used to indicate two things or people—and *only* two. *Among* is used to indicate three or more. Here's an example: *The teacher shared the crayons between the students.* Implicitly, the teacher only has two students. If he has more than two students, to be correct the sentence must read: *The teacher shared the crayons among the students.*

Bring/Take

Here's a question—do you bring something to a party or do you take something to a party? It's a dilemma. Before you can choose between *bring* and *take*, you must first establish where the speaker is or will be, even if it means playing with the sentence a little bit.

In order for the correct choice to be *bring*, the object in question must be going to or along with the speaker. Here's an example:

You and your best friend have been invited to a potluck dinner. Since you obviously don't want to arrive with the same dish, you ask her *What are you going to bring to the party?* In this case, *bring* is the correct choice because you, the speaker, are going to be at the party as well.

Assume, however, that you wake up on the day of the party too sick to attend. You are in charge of dessert, and no dinner party is complete without dessert. So you call your best friend and ask her *Will you take the dessert with you tonight?* In this case, she is *taking* the dessert because the dessert is going away from you, the speaker. If she is a good friend, she will also *bring* you, the speaker, aspirin for you headache and hot tea for your throat.

Remember, bring along with or to the speaker and take away from the speaker.

Could Of/Would Of/ Should Of

This is one example of ways people can be lazy with their speech. Nearly everyone has used one of the above phrases at some point in time. They are, however, all incorrect. Instead of writing *could of*, write *could have*. It was using the contraction "could've" and slurring the "have" at the end of the full phrase "could have" that developed the incorrect one in the first place. Therefore, instead of writing *She would of agreed to babysit if she hadn't had to study that night*, be sure to write *She would have agreed to babysit if she hadn't had to study that night*. "Should have" is perfectly acceptable. "Should of" is perfectly wrong.

Except/Accept

Since these two words are pronounced so similarly, it is often hard to tell them apart when they are spoken. This has led to confusion around which word is used at which time. *Except* means to exclude or excluding. *Everyone went to the party except John, who had to work that night.* On the other hand, *accept* means to respond favorably to something or to understand something is common or normal. *John's roommate accepted the invitation in John's place. This happened so often that it was an accepted practice for the roommates to attend parties in each others' stead.* They're easy to confuse.

Flammable/Inflammable

This one seems easy. The prefix *in* tends to mean "not." There's correct and incorrect, frequent and infrequent, separable and inseparable. So what's the problem? You have heard the saying, "There's an exception to every rule." *Flammable* and *inflammable* are the exception to the "in means not" rule.

Flammable means quick to burn or flame. Inflammable means quick to burn or flame. Instead of being antonyms as they would appear to be, they are actually synonyms. Feel free to interchange these two all you wish.

Hung/Hanged

You were probably taught that "hanged" is incorrect. That the past tense of hang is hung. That is true except under one condition. When discussing the old-time style of execution, the criminal is hanged. *The little girl hung her brother over the railing* is correct. *The cattle rustler was hanged at dawn* is also correct.

Irregardless

Irregardless is not actually a word. Yes, it is in common use. And yes, it has become so commonly used that it is now in the dictionary. It is however generally marked as informal or slang. When people say "irregardless," what they mean is "regardless." Since *regardless* means in spite of everything or anyway, just use *regardless*. That's the word you really want. As for *irregardless*, just don't use it. Ever.

Lose/Loose

Somewhere along the line, these two words became confused in many people's writings. But their meanings are very different. They are even pronounced differently so this confusion cannot be explained away by the way they sound when they are spoken as is the case with some of the other examples. *Lose* means to misplace. *Loose* means not tight.

Prefix/Prefixes

I want to draw attention to this particular question because of the appendix/appendices note above. Remember in the opening statement of this appendix, it was noted that the English language is a complex one? Here is an excellent example of that. It would seem logical that if there is debate over the plural of *appendix* then there would be debate over the plural of *prefix*. However, there is not. The plural of *prefix* is, in fact, *prefixes*.

Stationary/Stationery

In the case of these two words, it isn't so much that people get them confused as it is many people simply do not know the second word even exists. They see *stationery* and think it is a misspelling of *stationary*. However, that is not the case. *Stationary* means staying still, not moving. *Stationery*, though, is the word that describes the paper on which letters are written.

Their/There/They're

All of us at some point in our lives have had to stop and think about this combination of words. Unfortunately, there is no magic trick to remembering which is which. You just have to memorize and remember. If something belongs to more than one person, it is *theirs*. *Whose car is it? It's their car.* When indicating placement, the word you want is *there*. *Where is the car? The car is over there.* The last one is the only one that can be played with a little because it is a contraction. If the phrase "they are" is appropriate, then you know *they're* is the correct choice. *Who is driving the car? They're driving the car.* Go slowly if this is one of your trouble spots.

Who/Whom

Many students get trapped into thinking that if they want to sound formal and educated, using *whom* is an easy way to succeed. Unfortunately, using *whom* incorrectly is also an easy way to look as if you don't quite know what you're talking about. The best trick to have up your sleeve when it comes to *who* and *whom* is to rework the sentence just a bit. Would it make sense to rephrase the sentence with a *to* in front of the word in question? If the question is *Who gave you the sweater?*, rewrite it as *To who gave you the sweater?* That just sounds silly. In this case, the correct word is *who*. However, if the question is *Who are you giving the sweater to?*, the rewrite would be *To whom are you giving the sweater?* That makes more sense. In this case, the correct word is *whom*. If the word *to* can logically be placed in front of the word, choose *whom*. Otherwise, stick with *who*.

Y'all

If you are from the northern half of the country, you may not even know this phrase. However, if you are from the southern half of the country, you are probably very familiar with it. *Y'all* (the contraction for *you all*) is used frequently in the southern states as a plural for you. It is, however, inappropriate in formal communication. Leave it out. Use *you* as the singular and *all* as the plural instead.

Four More Common Mistakes

If you understand words and grammar—and the SAT and GRE testers do!—certain common mistakes can be the bane of your existence. Here we'll briefly touch on four of the most common ones: apostrophes, the word *at*, double negatives, and quotation marks. Avoiding these mistakes will increase your essay scores and endear you to the testers.

Apostrophes

First and foremost, making a singular into a plural does not require using an apostrophe. Apostrophes are used only to indicate possession or in a contraction. For example, you may see a sign in a store that reads: *Checks accepted with proper identification.* This is correct. They accept checks. They accept lots of checks, so long as everyone has proper ID. And nothing belongs to the checks. There is no possession in the sentence, therefore there should be no apostrophe. Here's another example: *The dog's leg was cut.* This is also correct. In the sentence, there is one dog and the leg belonging—possessed by—the dog is cut.

When writing about two or more people or things that possess something, the apostrophe is placed *after* the *s*. Therefore, the sentence would read: *The dogs' leashes were tangled.* There are two dogs. They each have a leash and those leashes were entwined.

You can often tell how many items are involved by where the apostrophe is placed. Take this sentence: *The fire hydrants' spray soaked the entire street.* According to this sentence, there is more than one fire hydrant spraying water. How can you tell that? Because the apostrophe is placed *after* the *s* at the end of the word. If the sentence read: *The fire hydrant's spray soaked the entire street,* you would know there was only one fire hydrant.

Avoid using contractions when writing a formal essay or document. Spell out both words.

While these rules may seem intimidating at first, they don't need to be. Just remember to ask yourself if the word is plural or possessive. If it is only plural, leave out the apostrophe. If it is possessive, add an apostrophe.

A quick word about *its* and *it's*: deciding whether or not to add an apostrophe to the word *it* seems to be one of the most difficult decisions for writers to make. When *it* becomes possessive, *do not use an apostrophe.* No possessive pronouns contain apostrophes—hers, his, theirs . . . its.

An apostrophe is only used for the contraction of *it is*. An easy reminder for test taking and other formal writing purposes is that you should never use an apostrophe with the word *it*. Either, *it* is possessive and thus has no apostrophe, or *it's* is a contraction of *it is* and thus you should spell it out.

At

When used correctly, the word *at* is a perfectly acceptable addition to a sentence. *The couple waited at the bar until their table was ready.* However, when used incorrectly, the word *at* will make testers—and anyone else who cares about grammar—cringe. Avoid using the word *at* at the end of a sentence at all costs. If you have lost a book and are asking about its location, the question is *Where is it?* The question is *not Where's it at?* It really is that easy.

Double Negatives

A double negative is a situation where *not* or another negative word is put in front of a word that already carries a negative connotation, such as "not inappropriate" or "can't hardly." This automatically creates a positive connotation but also creates confusion. While this may have its place in informal or stylized writing, it is inappropriate in formal writing. In the above examples, you would use "appropriate" and "hardly" instead. Both are more concise and far clearer to your reader.

Quotation Marks

Everyone knows to use quotation marks when citing a source or quoting a person directly. Quotation marks can also be used around a single word, but they should not be used for emphasis. It has become common practice to put quotation marks around *any* word that needs emphasis. This is incorrect. To stress a word, italicize or underline it.

Quotation marks used around a single word or phrase indicate this word is being used to indicate a different definition than the word usually carries. Consider it the "wink, wink," inside joke indicator of punctuation. Let's take a sentence and break it down.

Did you meet her friend, Brandon, at the party?

Written like that, it is straightforward. The woman in question has a friend named Brandon, and Brandon was at a party.

However, add strategic quotation marks and the sentence takes on a whole new meaning:

Did you meet her "friend" Brandon at the party?

The quotation marks indicate that the speaker means something other than the standard definition of the word *friend*, and the meaning of the question changes slightly. Perhaps everyone knows or suspects the woman and Brandon are dating but she continues to try to hide it, introducing him only as her friend. Perhaps Brandon is actually her biggest rival at work and she only invited him hoping to get some dirt on him. Whatever the situation, the quotation marks indicate Brandon is something other than a friend.

Appendix C

Frequently Misused Words, or But I Thought It Meant . . .

Many, many words in the English language are misused on a daily basis. Using key words correctly, however, can make you stand out in college interviews, job interviews, and any other time you want to prove you are well educated. Here are four of the most commonly misused words, their correct definitions, and an explanation of how to avoid misusing them again. They also happen to be, surprisingly enough, words you stand a very good chance of coming across on a test.

Aggravate

In casual conversation, using "aggravate" synonymously as "annoy" is perfectly acceptable. In formal situations, they should not be used interchangeably. Use "aggravate" when you mean to make an already bad situation worse. Use "annoy" if you mean to irritate. So, if you are having a really bad day to begin with, the obnoxiously loud person on the subway does indeed aggravate the situation. However, if you are having a delightful day, the same person behaving the same way is annoying, not aggravating. Scratching may aggravate a rash by spreading it and making it worse. A mosquito is annoying. Generally speaking in formal writing and speech, situations become aggravated. A person becomes annoyed.

Ambivalent

A surprising number of people do not understand what *ambivalent* truly means. Yes, it is difficult to make a decision when one is ambivalent. However, most people believe it is difficult to make that decision because the person is indifferent or doesn't care one way or another about the outcome. In reality, the exact opposite is true. To be ambivalent is to care deeply about two options or outcomes that are at odds with one another. A woman who wants to marry the man she loves but does not want the responsibility of entwining her life with another's is ambivalent. A man who has been offered a dream job 5,000 miles away from his elderly parents who need his care is ambivalent. Thus, ambivalence occurs when both options carry very high stakes and the person cares deeply about both. It is never used as a synonym for indifference.

Ironic

Interestingly enough, *ironic* and its different forms are used correctly as often as they are used incorrectly. Something is ironic when it is poignantly unexpected, highlights human inconsistencies, or teaches a lesson about human nature. And what in the world does that mean? What it means is that a coincidence, even a poignant one, is just a coincidence. An ironic situation is one that moves us deeply by the unexpected and often unfair result.

Something to watch for—if there is no expectation or lesson involved, there is no irony. If a man meets a woman randomly and then discovers she is married, it is not ironic because there was no reason to expect her to be single. If, on the other hand, the same man goes out and meets a woman for the purpose of a one-night hookup, falls in love with her, and then discovers she is married and leaving town at the end of the week—that's irony. First, he had reason to expect her to be single. Second, there was a lesson about human nature: All he was looking for was a hookup and instead he found a love he couldn't have.

Irony is a tough concept to grasp. Your quick fix is to ask yourself *Was there an expectation? Was there a lesson in human nature?* If the answer to either of those questions is yes, go with irony. If not, stick with coincidence.

Peruse

Peruse has come to be used the same way the phrases *to skim* or *to glance at briefly* are used. These, however, are incorrect definitions. Peruse is actually defined exactly oppositely. If you peruse something, you read it carefully, cover to cover. You may skim a menu but you probably won't peruse it, regardless of what your server says. Perusing contracts before signing them is, on the other hand, a very good idea. When writing or speaking, be sure to use the correct definition, not the common one.

Appendix D

Tips for Avoiding Test-Taking Jitters

Everyone gets nervous leading up to an important event, and however much you may wish otherwise, the SAT and the GRE are important events. Your scores affect what school you'll attend next, what scholarships will be available to you, even possibly what jobs you will get in the future. Plus, you cared enough to pick up at least one book as a study guide. Don't be ashamed or embarrassed to admit this is important to you—important enough to give you the jitters.

As a public speaker and trainer, I am *very* familiar with butterflies in the stomach, jitters, nerves, whatever you want to call them. I have also seen—and experienced—how nerves can throw off even the best prepared person. In order to help you avoid being controlled by your nerves, this appendix offers some tried-and-true, yet very simple, ideas that might help you relax. The more relaxed you are, the better your brain will deliver for you during the test itself.

The evening before:

1. Do not cram. If you need or want to look over one or two things, fine. Do that. But when your teachers used to tell you if you don't know it by now you won't know it for the test, they were right. Don't open the books at all the night before. If you must, look over one or two trouble spots, and then close the books.
2. Do something you enjoy. The goal here is to take your mind off tomorrow's test. You know yourself best so do what fits you. If you

are an athlete, go for a run, shoot hoops, get together a pick up game of football. If you do best with less physical activities, take a hot bath, veg in front of the television, play computer games. Whatever suits your needs.

3. If you are a drinker, do not get a buzz on. The last thing you need tomorrow is a hangover.

4. Make sure everything you will need tomorrow is ready. Are all your papers and pencils in one place? Do you need a specific ticket or ID to get into the test? Make sure everything is ready to go for the morning. That way, you won't have to run around at the last minute. Be sure to take a light sweater or jacket. Many testing sites are air-conditioned. Have something to put on in case you get cold.

5. Get to sleep at a decent hour. This is not a night to go out dancing all night with your girlfriends, even if that would distract you. Start winding down earlier than usual so that when it comes time to go to bed, you will get to sleep instead of lying there, staring at the ceiling. That gives you more time to stress about the test. Try to get no less than seven hours of sleep, more if you know you need it.

The morning of:

1. Set the alarm a little earlier than you know you need to get up. Today is not the day to be rushed or running late. Plan on getting to the testing site a little early in order to have time to get settled in before it's time to begin the test.

2. Don't open your study guides. It's always tempting to just check one last thing or only review this one section. Let it go. It's okay.

3. Have breakfast. Even if you don't usually eat in the mornings, do so today. If you aren't used to food this early, have something small. A piece of toast along with your coffee or tea is enough. Just make sure your body has fuel to burn over the next several hours.

4. Wear comfortable clothing. No one cares how you look. I promise. Yes, you should shower and brush your teeth. But don't worry about making sure the jacket matches the heels matches the jewelry. If you are not comfortable without makeup, wear makeup. If you are comfortable in sweats and a T-shirt, wear sweats and a T-shirt. Again, this is about you and what works for you, not anyone else. It will, however,

be difficult to concentrate if you are physically uncomfortable.

5. If you are allowed to have drinks in the testing room, take something with you to drink. I recommend water but I know that some people just don't drink it. Take something to help counter dry mouth and the distracting cough that can result.

During the test:

1. Find a seat where you will be comfortable. If you are easily distracted, stay away from the windows. If you get cold easily, avoid sitting near the air-conditioning units, or sit close to the heating ducts, depending on the time of year.

2. Once you have claimed your seat, make one last run to the restroom. Our bodies react to stress in ways we might consider odd. One of the ways many people react is by having to go the bathroom once the stress kicks in. Save yourself that concern. Along those lines . . . .

3. If you were allowed to bring a drink into the room (some test sites allow it, some do not) keep your drink close by but only sip at it. One of the greatest distractions is realizing you need a break and not being able to take one. Keep your mind on your test and not your bladder by monitoring your fluid intake.

4. If you are a smoker, buy a box of nicotine patches to wear today. Brand doesn't matter. What matters is that you get through the test without a debilitating nic-fit!

5. Don't forget to breathe. I know this one sounds crazy but people do honestly forget to breathe when they get nervous. Instead of taking deep breaths, many people often take very small, very shallow breaths. The brain won't work if it's not getting enough oxygen. If you need help settling down, try this: Put the palms of your hands together in front of your chest. Now, push them together. The body's natural reaction to that motion is to exhale and relax. Once you have gotten to this point, take a deep breath in. Hold it for a count of three and let it back out again. There. You are back to breathing normally. And for the record, this movement will also lower your voice if you are speaking and discover you are getting squeaky. I have no idea why any of this works. I only know it does.

After the test:

Celebrate! All your hard work has paid off and you have finished the test! It's out of the way, over and done. There is no reason to stress over the results. They will be what they are and it'll be several weeks before you get them anyway. For today, pat yourself on the back. You deserve it!

Word List

abbreviate	aberrant	abet
abeyance	abjure	ablution
abridge	abrogate	abscond
abstemious	abstinence	abstract
abstruse	abut	accede
accessible	acclaim	accolade
acerbic	acquiesce	acrid
acrimony	acumen	adage
adamant	admonition	adulation
adulterate	adumbrate	adversary
adversity	advocate	aesthetic
affable	affirmation	aggravate
aggregate	agile	agog
alchemy	alcove	alleviate
aloof	altruistic	ambidextrous
ambiguous	ambivalence	amenable
amicable	amorphous	anachronistic
analogous	anarchist	anecdote
anomaly	anonymous	antagonist
antediluvian	antidote	antiquated
antithesis	apathy	aplomb
apogee	apostate	apotheosis
apparition	appease	apposite
apprehension	apprise	approbation
arable	arbitrary	arboreal
archaic	argot	arid
arrant	arrogance	articulate

artifact	artisan	ascendancy
ascetic	asperity	aspire
assiduous	assuage	astringent
astute	asylum	atonement
atrophy	attribute	audacious
augury	austere	authoritarian
autocrat	autonomous	auxiliary
aver	aversion	avert
aviary	avow	axiom
baleful	balm	banal
bask	beatify	bedaub
beguile	belie	benefactor
benevolent	benign	berate
bewilder	blandishment	blatant
bleak	blighted	blithe
boisterous	bolster	braggart
breach	brevity	brittle
broach	bucolic	bumptious
bouyant	burgeon	burnish
buttress	cabal	cacophony
cajole	calculated	callow
calumny	camaraderie	candid
candor	canon	capacious
capitulate	captious	cardiologist
carping	castigation	catalyst
cataract	caustic	censorious
censure	centurion	certitude
charlatan	chary	circuitous
clairvoyant	clarity	cliché
coalesce	coddle	coercion
coeval	cogent	cogitate
cognizant	coherent	collaborate
colloquial	combustible	comestible
commemorate	compassion	compile
complacency	complacent	complaisance

complement	compliance	comport
composure	comprehensive	compromise
concede	conceit	conciliatory
concise	concord	concur
condense	condescending	conditional
condone	conflagration	confluence
conformist	confound	congeal
congenital	congregation	conjoin
connoisseur	consensus	console
conspicuous	consternation	constraint
constrict	contemptuous	contend
contentious	contiguous	contract
contrite	contumacious	convention
convergence	conviction	cordial
cornucopia	corporeal	correlate
corrode	corrugated	counterfeit
countervail	covet	cower
crass	credulity	criterion
cryptic	culminate	cursory
curtail	cynicism	cynosure
dearth	debunk	decimate
decorum	defer	degradation
dehydrate	deign	deleterious
deluge	demagogue	denizen
dénouement	denounce	deplete
deplore	depose	deposition
deprave	deride	derision
derivative	descry	desiccated
desuetude	desultory	detached
deterrent	detrimental	devious
devise	dexterity	diaphanous
diffuse	digression	dilate
dilatory	dilettante	diligence
disabuse	disallow	discern
disclose	discomfit	disconsolate

discordant	discount	discountenance
discourse	discredit	discreet
discrepancy	discretion	discriminating
disdain	disheveled	disinclination
disinterested	dismiss	disparate
disputation	disquiet	dissemble
dissent	dissolution	distend
distraught	divergent	divest
divulge	doctrine	document
dormant	dubious	dupe
duplicity	earthenware	eccentric
eclectic	edacious	edible
educe	efface	effervesce
effete	efficacy	effulgence
egotism	egress	elated
elegy	elicit	elusive
emaciate	embellish	embezzle
emblazon	emend	emollient
empathy	empirical	emulate
encomium	encumbrance	endorse
engender	engrave	enhance
enigma	ennui	entangle
entreat	ephemeral	epithet
epitome	equable	equilibrium
equine	equitable	equivocal
equiviocate	eradicate	errant
erratic	erroneous	erudite
eschew	espy	eulogy
euphemism	euphonious	evince
evoke	exalt	exasperation
excerpt	execute	exemplary
exemplify	exhaustive	exhilarating
exigent	exorbitant	expatiate
expedient	expedite	expiate
explicate	explicit	exploit

expostulate	expropriate	extant
extemporaneous	extenuating	extinct
extinguish	extirpate	extol
extort	extraneous	extricate
exuberance	facetious	facile
facilitate	factious	fallacious
fallacy	fallow	falter
fanaticism	fathom	fawn
feasible	feint	fell
felon	ferocity	fervent
fervid	fervor	fidelity
filibuster	finesse	fitful
flagrant	flamboyant	flippant
florid	flout	fluidly
foment	foolhardy	foppish
forbearance	forfeit	forgery
forswear	fortuitous	fragile
frantic	frivolous	frugality
fugacious	fulminate	fulsome
furtive	gainsay	gamut
germane	gesticulate	glacial
glib	glimmer	glutton
gossamer	gourmand	grandiloquence
gratify	gratuitous	gravity
grievous	gullible	halcyon
hamper	harangue	hardy
haughtiness	headlong	hedonist
hegemony	heinous	heresy
heretical	heterogenous	hirsute
homogeneous	hoodwink	hospitable
hubris	hypocritical	hypothetical
idiosyncrasy	idolatrous	ignoble
illicit	illusory	imbroglio
imbue	immaculate	imminent
immutable	impair	impassive

impeccable	impecunious	impede
imperative	imperturbable	impervious
impetus	impiety	implacable
implausible	implement	implicate
implicit	importunate	importune
impregnable	impromptu	improvident
impudence	impunity	impute
inadvertently	inane	inchoate
incidental	incisive	incite
inclusive	incompatible	incongruous
inconsequential	incorrigible	incredulity
indelible	indict	indifferent
indigenous	indigent	indiscriminate
indistinct	indolence	indomitable
induce	indulgent	ineffable
ineluctable	inept	inert
inevitable	infelicitous	infuse
ingénue	ingenuous	inherent
inimical	innate	innocuous
innovation	inscrutable	insensible
insinuate	insipid	insolvent
insouciant	instigate	insularity
insuperable	insurrection	integrity
interim	intervene	intimidate
intractable	intransigent	intrepid
introspection	intuitive	inundate
inure	invalid	inveigh
inveigle	invert	inveterate
invidious	invincible	iota
irascible	irate	ire
irksome	ironic	irreproachable
itinerant	itinerate	jocular
jovial	jubilation	judiciously
junta	kinetic	kith
knobbly	kohl	kowtow

labyrinth	lachrymose	lackadaisical
lament	lampoon	lascivious
lassitude	latent	laudable
laudatory	lavish	legacy
lenient	lethargic	levee
levity	lexicon	libel
licentious	lien	linger
listless	lithe	lobbyist
lofty	longevity	loquacious
lucid	luminary	lurid
lustrous	luxuriant	malcontent
malevolent	malicious	malign
malleable	manifest	manumit
mar	martial	maudlin
maverick	mawkish	meander
mellifluous	mendacity	mendicant
mercenary	meretricious	mesmerize
meticulous	mettle	mettlesome
microcosm	mien	mirth
misanthrope	mischievous	miscreant
miser	miserly	misnomer
mitigate	moderation	modicum
mollify	molt	monolithic
monomania	mordant	morose
mosaic	multifarious	munificent
myriad	nadir	nascent
nebulous	nefarious	neologism
noisome	nominal	nostrum
notoriety	nugatory	obdurate
obfuscate	obstreperous	obtrude
obviate	odious	odium
officious	ominous	onus
opportunist	opprobrium	orator
ornate	oscillate	ossify
ostracism	ostracize	pacifist

paean	palate	palatial
palliate	palpable	panacea
panegyric	panapoly	pariah
paroxysm	partisan	pathos
peccadillo	pedagogy	pedantic
pellucid	penchant	penurious
penury	peregrination	peremptory
perennial	perfidy	perfunctory
peripatetic	peripheral	permeate
pernicious	perpetuate	persiflage
perturbation	peruse	pervade
pessimism	petrified	petulant
phenomena	philanthropist	phlegmatic
physiognomy	piety	pious
pique	pitfall	pith
platitude	plenary	plethora
plumb	polyglot	ponderous
portent	pragmatic	prattle
precarious	precedent	precipitate
preclude	precocious	precursor
predator	predecessor	predilection
preen	presage	pretentious
preternatural	prevalent	prevaricate
probity	proclivity	procrastination
prodigal	prodigious	profane
profligacy	profuse	proliferation
prolific	prolix	propensity
propitious	prosaic	proscribe
prosperity	protuberant	provident
provincial	provocative	proximity
prudence	punctilious	pungent
pusillanimous	putrefy	pyre
quaff	qualm	quandary
quell	query	quibble
quiescent	quotidian	raconteur

ramify	rancor	rapacious
rarefy	raucous	raze
reactionary	rebuff	rebuttal
recant	reciprocal	reciprocity
recondite	recrudescent	rectify
redoubtable	redress	refractory
refulgent	refute	regicide
reiterate	relegate	remonstrate
remorse	renege	renounce
repast	repine	reprehensible
reprove	repudiate	requisite
requite	rescind	resilient
resolution	resonance	resplendent
restrained	retinue	retract
reverence	reverent	rigor
risible	robust	rotund
ruffian	sage	salacious
salient	salubrious	salutary
sanction	sardonic	satiate
saturate	satyr	savor
savory	scabbard	scanty
scintilla	scrupulous	seclusion
sedentary	sedition	sedulous
servile	severance	shard
sinecure	sinuous	skeptic
skiff	sluggard	sluggish
solace	solicitous	solvent
somniferous	somnolent	sonorous
sophistry	soporific	specious
spurn	squalid	stagnation
stigma	stoic	stolid
strident	stupefy	stymie
subordinate	subpoena	subside
substantiate	subterfuge	sumptuous
supercilious	superfluous	supernumerary

supersede	supine	supplant
supplicate	surcharge	surfeit
sybarite	synthesis	taciturn
tantamount	temerity	tentative
tenuous	terrestrial	terse
timorous	torpid	torpor
torque	torrid	tout
tractable	transient	transitory
travesty	trenchant	trifling
truculence	truculent	truncate
turbid	turgid	turmoil
turpitude	tutelage	tyro
ulterior	undulate	untenable
untoward	unwarranted	upbraid
usurp	vagary	vainglory
valorous	vapid	variegated
vehement	venal	vendetta
veneer	venerable	venial
veracious	verbiage	verbose
verdant	veritable	vestige
vexation	vicissitude	vigilant
vilify	vindicate	virago
virtu	virtuoso	visage
viscous	vitiate	vituperate
vituperative	vivify	vociferous
voluble	wary	wean
whimsical	witticism	xenophobia
xerophyte	xylography	xylophagous
yare	yearling	yen
yeti	yew	zealot
zeitgeist